Kitchens
and
Gadgets

1920 to 1950

Jane H. Celehar

Photographs: Ed Johnson
Pro Media
Columbus, Ohio

ISBN 0-87069-358-1
Library of Congress Catalog
Card Number 80-53301

10 9

Published by

Wallace-Homestead

Wallace-Homestead Book Company
201 King of Prussia Road
Radnor, Pennsylvania 19089

Contents

Acknowledgments

I wish to express my gratitude to my family and all my friends for their support, suggestions, and generous help. My thanks also to all the people who have allowed me to use their magazines, catalogs, and other items that were necessary for the research of this book. It has been a rewarding experience to have had the opportunity to form so many new friendships resulting from the pursuit of this project.

To all the librarians for their valuable assistance, I am most appreciative.

An unbelievable chain of contacts resulted in pertinent information which was vital for the history of various companies and other related data.

My appreciation is extended to all the magazines and companies for their cooperation and resources and for the interest of their employees—many of whom added personal observations.

A special thank you to the Ekco Housewares Company who offered me the opportunity to do research with the A & J and Ekco catalogs from the 1920s to 1950s and provided the reproduced catalog pages which appear in the book.

This book would not have been possible without the cooperation of so many people whose interest, time, and resources were made available to me. I want to thank each of them.

Introduction

Collecting green handled kitchen tools and gadgets encouraged my search for more knowledge about them. The lack of printed information on these items from the 1920s and 1930s led me into extensive research.

Researching these kitchen collectibles has been work, fun, interesting, and extremely rewarding. It was hard to know where to begin to gather facts about the manufacturers and their products. At times it became very discouraging because of unanswered inquiries and other closed avenues of approach. People made the difference!

Each new discovery, whether it be a new approach, source, answered query, or identification of a "whatsit," spurred me on with excitement. It was like solving a mystery, finding each piece and then finally fitting all the pieces together. The information gathered about green handled items also provided data about tools and gadgets with wooden handles of other colors.

Research also led me to look further into the room where these tools were used — the *kitchen* itself. Seeing what tremendous changes have occurred in the kitchen during this era widened my investigation to include a history of it during this time.

The photographs of approximately 550 different items in this book will help the reader in identifying and dating and will additionally provide miscellaneous related data and current values. To facilitate printing, all trademarks are shown in a separate listing rather than with the individual description.

The chapter on the history of the manufacturers includes every company whose name is marked on the illustrated items. Histories are not available for all manufacturers since many small companies who produced kitchenware during this time have been dissolved or acquired by larger concerns, making them hard to trace. I would welcome any additional information from my readers.

There is a great deal of nostalgic interest in the past. Hopefully this glimpse of bygone days will renew memories for those whose lives touched this era, stimulate the imaginations of others, and provide helpful information for the collector of kitchenware.

Kitchen tools and gadgets from the 1920–1950 period are still available collectibles today. In this day of "plastic," kitchen items from the past are fun, interesting to collect, and decorative, not to mention durable and useful.

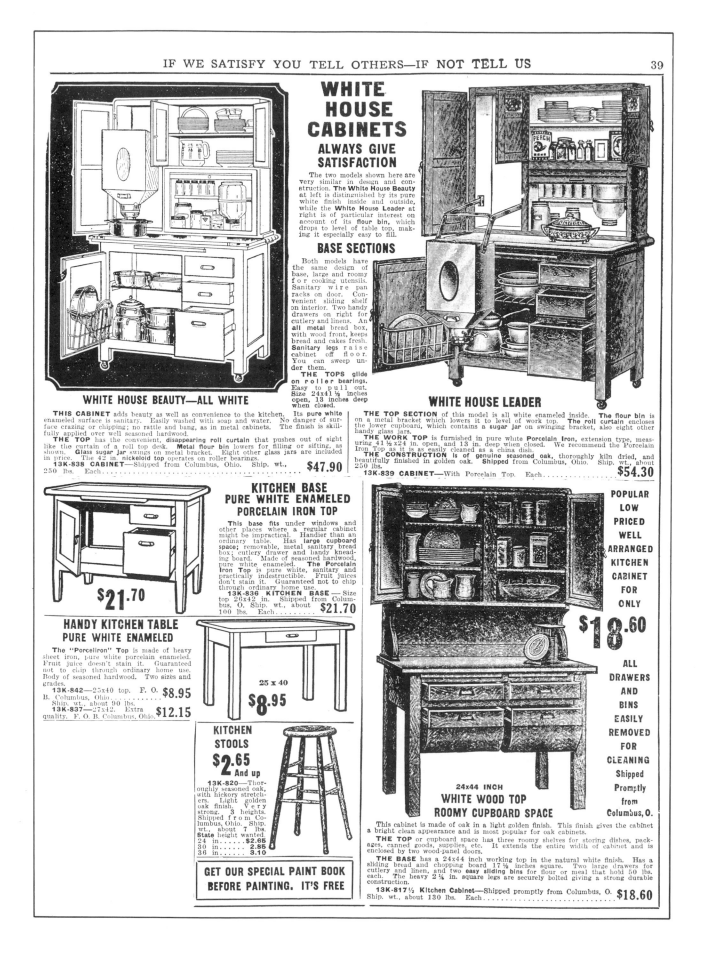

WHITE HOUSE CABINETS

ALWAYS GIVE SATISFACTION

The two models shown here are very similar in design and construction. **The White House Beauty** at left is distinguished by its pure white finish inside and outside, while the **White House Leader** at right is of particular interest on account of its **flour bin**, which drops to level of table top, making it especially easy to fill.

BASE SECTIONS

Both models have the same design of base, large and roomy for cooking utensils. Sanitary wire pan racks on door. Convenient sliding shelf on interior. Two handy drawers on right for cutlery and linens. An **all metal bread box**, with wood front, keeps bread and cakes fresh. **Sanitary legs raise** cabinet off floor. You can sweep under them.

THE TOPS glide on roller bearings. Easy to pull out. Size 24x41½ inches open, 13 inches deep when closed.

WHITE HOUSE BEAUTY—ALL WHITE

THIS CABINET adds beauty as well as convenience to the kitchen. Its pure white enameled surface is sanitary. Easily washed with soap and water. No danger of surface crazing or chipping; no rattle and bang, as in metal cabinets. The finish is skillfully applied over well seasoned hardwood.
THE TOP has the convenient, disappearing roll curtain that pushes out of sight like the curtain of a roll top desk. Metal flour bin lowers for filling or sifting, as shown. **Glass sugar Jar** swings on metal bracket. Eight other glass jars are included in price. The 42 in. nickeloid top operates on roller bearings.
13K-838 CABINET—Shipped from Columbus, Ohio. Ship. wt., 250 lbs. Each.................... **$47.90**

WHITE HOUSE LEADER

THE TOP SECTION of this model is all white enameled inside. The flour bin is on a metal bracket which lowers it to level of work top. The roll curtain encloses the lower cupboard, which contains a **sugar jar** on swinging bracket, also eight other handy glass jars.
THE WORK TOP is furnished in pure white Porcelain Iron, extension type, measuring 41½ x24 in. open, and 13 in. deep when closed. We recommend the Porcelain Iron Top as it is as easily cleaned as a china dish.
THE CONSTRUCTION is of genuine seasoned oak, thoroughly kiln dried, and beautifully finished in golden oak. Shipped from Columbus, Ohio. Ship. wt., about 250 lbs.
13K-839 CABINET—With Porcelain Top. Each................. **$54.30**

KITCHEN BASE
PURE WHITE ENAMELED PORCELAIN IRON TOP

This base fits under windows and other places where a regular cabinet might be impractical. Handier than an ordinary table. Has **large cupboard** space; removable, metal sanitary bread box; cutlery drawer and handy kneading board. Made of seasoned hardwood, pure white enameled. **The Porcelain Iron Top** is pure white, sanitary and practically indestructible. Fruit juices don't stain it. Guaranteed not to chip through ordinary home use.
13K-836 KITCHEN BASE— Size top 26x42 in. Shipped from Columbus, O. Ship. wt., about 100 lbs. Each........ **$21.70**

$21.70

HANDY KITCHEN TABLE
PURE WHITE ENAMELED

The "Porceliron" Top is made of heavy sheet iron, pure white porcelain enameled. Fruit juice doesn't stain it. Guaranteed not to chip through ordinary home use. Body of seasoned hardwood. Two sizes and grades.
13K-842—25x40 top. F. O. B. Columbus, Ohio........... **$8.95** Ship. wt., about 90 lbs.
13K-837—27x42. Extra quality. F. O. B. Columbus, Ohio. **$12.15**

25 x 40

$8.95

KITCHEN STOOLS

$2.65 And up

13K-820—Thoroughly seasoned oak, with hickory stretchers. Light golden oak finish. Very strong. 3 heights. Shipped from Columbus, Ohio. Ship. wt., about 7 lbs. State height wanted.
24 in.....$2.65
30 in..... 2.85
36 in..... 3.10

GET OUR SPECIAL PAINT BOOK BEFORE PAINTING. IT'S FREE

POPULAR LOW PRICED WELL ARRANGED KITCHEN CABINET FOR ONLY

$18.60

ALL DRAWERS AND BINS EASILY REMOVED FOR CLEANING Shipped Promptly from Columbus, O.

24x44 INCH
WHITE WOOD TOP
ROOMY CUPBOARD SPACE

This cabinet is made of oak in a light golden finish. This finish gives the cabinet a bright clean appearance and is most popular for oak cabinets.
THE TOP or cupboard space has three roomy shelves for storing dishes, packages, canned goods, supplies, etc. It extends the entire width of cabinet and is enclosed by two wood-panel doors.
THE BASE has a 24x44 inch working top in the natural white finish. Has a sliding bread and chopping board 17½ inches square. Two large drawers for cutlery and linen, and two **easy sliding bins** for flour or meal that hold 50 lbs. each. The heavy 2¼ in. square legs are securely bolted giving a strong durable construction.
13K-817½ Kitchen Cabinet—Shipped promptly from Columbus, O. Ship. wt., about 130 lbs. Each.......................... **$18.60**

American Kitchens 1920 to 1950

The kitchen, "the heart of the house" today, was the stepchild of the house in years past. No longer separated from the house as in colonial days, or hidden away in the basement as in the Victorian era, today's kitchen has emerged as the most used and the most important room in the American home. It is fascinating to see the changes that took place through the years to produce the kitchen as we now know it.

At the turn of the century, the kitchen was dull and drab, hidden somewhere in the back of the house, and seen only by servants. The large, dark, and inefficient room was to become the smaller "sanitary" kitchen of the 1920s. This slow evolution would undergo dramatic changes between World War I and World War II. Until this time, the kitchen had changed less than any other room in the house. Since then, no other room has been more completely researched and analyzed.

Domestic pioneers such as Catherine Beecher (in the mid-1800s) elevated housekeeping to a science by organizing the kitchen with efficient, laborsaving plans. She addressed the "servant (live-in) help" problem when she directed attention to the contradiction of a "permanent serving class" existing in a democratic society. In the early 1900s an awareness of the relationship between the servant and employer again surfaced. It was realized that serving class, domestic workers were considered inferior to other working people.

After 1910, domestic scientists were able to capture public attention for the efficient kitchen. The fitted cabinet was the first step in modernizing the old-fashioned kitchen, replacing the open shelves which collected dust. It was a spacesaving, movable, efficient cabinet with a place for everything—handy containers,

1. Fitted kitchen cabinets were featured in a Cussins & Fearn Company catalog in 1921.

pullout workshelf, sifter and flour bin, drawers, and cupboard shelves.

During the 1920s and 1930s, lifestyles were changing; the kitchen reflected these social changes. The already existent servant problem became acute during and after World War I as factories attracted domestic workers with the promise of higher pay, shorter hours, and independence. The kitchen took on new importance as housewives found they had to spend more and more time doing menial tasks. Some estimated 70 percent of their working hours were spent this way.

The shortage of household help required solutions. There was a great demand for any laborsaving device. Any new idea or gadget which promised to make the kitchen more convenient and food preparation less time-consuming was quickly grasped. Advertising, the quick and direct way to stimulate mass consumption, helped to improve the home by telling the housewife about these new "servants." The desire to relieve the constant drudgery of housework provoked the invention of devices designed to improve household organization and to emancipate the housewife.

The kitchen underwent great changes in the 1920 and 1930s. The principles used by industry to organize the work process (the assembly line and scientific management) were, one by one, applied to the household. During this twenty-year period, according to Sigfried Giedion, more appliances developed into household necessities than had been seen in the whole preceding century. The entry of mass-produced goods into the home freed women from such traditional jobs as canning and breadmaking. As mechanization and efficiency increased, the size of the kitchen decreased.

The sanitary kitchen of the 1920s was all white, with every inch of space finished so that it could be scrubbed. It was sterile and devoid of imagination. Linoleum or a similar practical floor covering (suggested because the wood floor collected dirt and germs in the gaps) was often the only note of color. The room contained separate furnishings—a sink on legs, a stove, a movable kitchen cabinet, a wooden or enameled work table, and an icebox.

Simplify, simplify. Save energy, save time, curtail household drudgery—all became familiar phrases in the press of the day. In 1912, Christine Frederick, author of *Household Engineering*, advocated a need for kitchen equipment to be standardized. She pointed to hotel kitchens where all the equipment was related. Hotels did not buy a table here and a stove there. She insisted that the home kitchen could also be made efficient with laborsaving equipment which was related and arranged according to a system of work.

It wasn't until 1923 that the kitchen furniture industry took the first step toward standardization by introducing steel cabinets, utility closets, and wall cabinets in different sizes and combinations and compartmentalized to hold everything from spices to brooms.

A kitchen which was planned for convenience saved steps. A time-motion study showed the number of steps required to bake a cake could be reduced from 281 to 45 by rearranging the equipment to follow the general order of work. The small items or utensils should be grouped conveniently around the work center, with preparation tools stored near the work table and cooking tools kept near the stove. Work could then proceed in a chain of steps, avoiding crisscrossing and fatigue. Proper height of the work center was also

2. The usual kitchen of the 1920s had separate furnishings, all at different heights.

3. One 1925 advertisement promoted standardized
kitchen cabinets.

4. These standardized cabinets were shown in
*Lazarus Cook Book & Kitchen Guide for the Busy
Woman,* 1932.

important because most drudgery was caused
by the "bends" (sinks set too low). The bends
also could be avoided with a foot-operated
garbage can.

By the mid-1920s, magazine articles urged
women to bring color into the kitchen. It was
stressed that a kitchen could be sanitary without resembling a hospital operating room and
that a colorful one was no harder to clean than
a white one. Dirt was dirt no matter what color
it appeared on. Glaring white kitchens were
hard on the eyes; an off-white or tan kitchen
was better. The use of pale green or blue or
whatever color suited the individual could
make it more cheerful. The food that came
from a sterile, white workroom may have been
good and nutritious, but there was a lot more
genuine enjoyment preparing it in a gay, colorful kitchen.

Macy's and Abraham & Strauss each
launched a campaign for "color in the kitchen"

in 1927. They offered housewares in coordinated colors of apple green, mandarin red, and
delft blue, including everything from paring
knives to canisters to tables. The industry was
amazed at the public response. The campaign

5. A foot-operated garbage can under a sink with
legs was popular in 1929.

6. When the first meal was cooked by electricity on the Red Wing experimental line in the Bennit Melin home, Melin was called to dinner before he finished his pipe. (Courtesy of General Electric Corporation.)

An American Queen's Kitchen of Today

PICTURE this kitchen of convenience, supplied with sunshine, air and water *ad lib*, painted a sunny yellow with black trimmings, and equipped with the best of working tools placed to one's hand—and then pity poor Sixteenth Century kings in their cavernous kitchens, where one had to run a mile to serve a meal!

Observe the sink under the window convenient to the closets for holding cleaning materials and brushes and putting away the washed pots and pans. The stove, always the hero of every kitchen drama, carries its oven high and requires no bending of the back before him. With the kitchen cabinet and its store of staple foods, seasonings, and small utensils to the left, the work table behind one, the closet of clean, large cooking utensils to the right and the sink a few steps away, one is ready to cook without also doing a marathon.

A long walk is a good thing—housekeepers should have more of them—but you don't want to take it in a hot kitchen when time is a consideration and a fixed meal hour must be met!

7. An ideal kitchen in 1927 had a stove with a high oven.

caught the imagination and appealed to women everywhere who were tired of the chaste white. "Color in the kitchen" offered a delightful spark of life to the monotonous, dreary room.

The stepchild of the house was now coming into its own, and for the first time it was being considered a vital part of the decorating scheme of the whole house. It was suggested that the kitchen be done in cool colors. Perhaps green was so popular because, as the color of grass, leaves, and vegetables, it suggested rest, cool shade, and refreshment. It was a unifying color that was considered beneficial to the eyes, nerves, and disposition. Blue was also a cool color, while yellow made a sparkling room. In contrast, red and orange were thought to be too intense, not restful.

The refrigerator, one of the joys of modern housekeeping, could be placed by the work center. It had been necessary for the old icebox to be near the door to eliminate the possibility of receiving footprints on the floor with each load of ice. The electric refrigerator was gaining in popularity. The number sold rose from 20,000 in 1923 to 850,000 in 1933. By 1936 sales increased to 2 million and totaled 3½ million by 1941.

384190   TYPE OC-2 FORM H REFRIGERATING MACHINE ON SEEGER NO. 375
REFRIGERATOR. DOORS OPEN.
APPROX. 1/12 SIZE   INDEX E-327   4 9 25

8. In 1925, this type of electric refrigerator was found in some homes. (Courtesy of General Electric Corporation.)

9. The late 1920s kitchen had no built-ins, but a separate pantry was not uncommon.

The problems of food spoilage, sickness caused by harmful bacteria, and loss of nutritional values were solved by mechanical refrigeration. Refrigerated transportation made it possible to have fresh fruits and vegetables, countrywide, year-round.

The vogue of breakfast nooks contributed to the kitchen's decorative importance. They were compact, spacesaving, and kept pace with the new trend of living styles of service. They were ideal for serving a quick breakfast or a late night snack and provided a touch of welcome and friendliness, making the kitchen a much more inviting room.

By 1930 the manufacturers of kitchen equipment focused on the work process by studying movement, charting steps, and arranging equipment in a more compact way. Kitchen

10. Breakfast areas were featured in the *Lazarus Cook Book & Kitchen Guide for the Busy Woman* in 1932.

planning was becoming important. Imagine how sleek and modern the built-in sink must have looked in 1930. Instead of a sink on four legs and a separate work table, the housewife was now offered a built-in unit with a continuous top connecting the base cabinets and the sink. Above this, separate wall cabinets could be installed.

11. The built-in sink, an integral part of cabinet and cupboard installations, was sunken into work surfaces. Doors with metal grates gave ventilation to the hidden plumbing. Both illustrations from *Better Homes and Gardens*, 1930s.

About this time gas companies recognized the trend started by the manufacturers of kitchen furniture. In 1930 Lillian Galbraith was commissioned by a gas company to study the kitchen as an industrial production problem. Studying movement and charting steps resulted in the rearrangement of equipment which transformed an unorganized area into an efficient, stepsaving compact room.

However, the available appliances were a chaotic mixture. Every manufacturer produced single units of different heights, depths, and levels, apparently without thought of the kitchens they were to occupy or attention to what other manufacturers were making. The realization came that organization was not enough; the kitchen had to be treated as a whole unit. So, in 1932, the electric companies began to set up special cooking institutes with engineers, architects, nutritionists, and cooks scientifically studying everything connected with the kitchen.

In 1931 the gas industry was first to attain the compact tabletop range which was the same height as other work surfaces. (It still had abbreviated legs.) This was the beginning of the integration of the range into the scheme of the modern kitchen.

By the mid-1930s, the electric companies followed suit. A range the same height as other work surfaces and proportioned to be continuous with base cabinets became standard form. By 1940 it turned on with a flip of a switch, and its oven selector regulated and maintained proper temperature.

The peak period to alleviate household drudgery, when kitchen planning reached a high state of perfection, was during the 1920s and 1930s. By 1935 basic planning principles were well established. These included the concept of work centers, ample storage, work surfaces, and careful placement of equipment to reduce floor space and save steps. Three main centers were now defined — storage, involving cupboards and refrigerator; food preparation, dishwashing, and cleaning, centering on the sink; and cooking and serving areas which were centered near the range. The sink was conveniently located between the refrigerator and the range. Around these three centers were grouped cabinets and accessories appropriate to each, with counters connecting them in a continuous working scheme, thus unifying all appliances with the work process and treating the kitchen as a harmonious whole. The streamlined kitchen was the product of these basic design principles.

Picture the "modern," streamlined kitchen of the thirties and forties. It was bright, cheerful, compact, and adequately equipped. There was a place for everything and everything was provided its most convenient place. The appearance of simplicity and balance was accomplished by the counters, range top, and sink at equal heights (36") from the floor, with the front surfaces of cabinets and appliances on an even plane. It was smartly styled and magically convenient, with equipment arranged continuously around the room to follow the order of work. The decorative scheme was according to individual taste.

It was possible to modernize an existing kitchen by planning and rearranging. An obviously large room could have the size reduced by creating a dining alcove or breakfast nook or by using surplus space for a pantry, storeroom, downstairs lavatory, or household office. Moving a partition to enlarge an adjoining dining or living room was another alternative. Sometimes satisfactory solutions could result from slight changes such as moving a radiator, adding a piece of pipe to better position a sink, or changing door hinges from one side to another.

To get the new, streamlined equipment, housewives could order complete ensembles or separate units from large corporations or mail order houses. The components could be combined several ways and were designed to fit other sections of the unit. The range, sink, refrigerator, and cabinets could be placed along one wall, two walls (L-shape), or three walls (U-shape). Various decorating possibilities were suggested.

Walls could be papered, painted, lined with linoleum, tile, or glass, or with one of many hard-surfaced, easily cleaned wall coverings. All of these were produced in a wide range of colors and patterns designed to harmonize with any decorative scheme.
Counters and sink tops were available in metal, wood, porcelain enamel, rubber, linoleum, and a durable composition which came in a variety of tones.

12. This G-E Chancellor electric range was popular in 1938. (Courtesy of General Electric Corporation.)

Cabinets were steel and customarily white, although units were available in colors. Wooden cabinets, which could be painted or used in natural wood tones, were also offered. **Windows** could have small shelves at their sides and curtains which contributed an important color note.

Lighting, in the form of attractive ceiling units, could be supplemented by shaded or concealed lights at points where work was done.

13. Space-saving cupboards and a stepsaving pass-through were featured in a 1930s kitchen. (Courtesy of Armstrong Cork Company.)

Architects, home economists, and cabinet and equipment manufacturers pooled their knowledge to develop the modern, streamlined kitchen. Industry then gave the advertising people the task of promoting the idea so that women would want good appliances and attractive kitchens. Housewives were receptive because of the change in lifestyles and their need for maximum efficiency and economy. Industry-wide advertising and promotion of the streamlined concept was so successful by the 1940s that most Americans were beginning to accept such a kitchen as the norm rather than the exception.

By this time a multitude of automatic and streamlined small electrical appliances were vying for shelf room and counter space in the kitchen. Homeowners were finding their home wiring inadequate to handle the stream of automatic toasters, irons, casseroles, roasters, electric corn poppers, waffle irons, mixers, and blenders which had found their way into their kitchens. Design of the postwar kitchen of the 1950s was specifically directed toward solving the problems of efficient storage of small appliances in a kitchen wired to power the combined tasks of food preparation, room ventilation, and clean-up in well lighted surroundings.

14. A bright dining corner highlighted a cozy 1930s kitchen. (Courtesy of Armstrong Cork Company.)

15.   Colorful and easy-to-clean flooring added appeal to the 1930s kitchen. (Courtesy of Armstrong Cork Company.)

In the 1930s large appliances such as the range and refrigerator were well established as standard equipment for the modern home.

Although the ideas were developed for the automatic clothes washer, garbage or waste disposal, electric dishwasher, and home freezer, none became immediate successes. Only when there is public acceptance of an appliance can mass production begin and the price become attractive. Automatic clothes washers were invented in the 1920s, but they weren't mass-marketed until 1939. Another example is the electric dishwasher, introduced in the 1920s, but still not commonly accepted by the late 1940s.

Canned and packaged foods had improved considerably, had become less expensive, and were offered in an ever-increasing variety by the 1940s. Easy-to-cook foods were becoming important. It took from the mid-1920s to 1940 for American housewives to appreciate the usefulness of frozen food. Once it gained acceptance, many decided it was just about the most convenient product to arrive in the kitchen.

16. Unique eating area in a 1930s kitchen also provided tidy organization for small kitchen appliances. (Courtesy of Armstrong Cork Company.)

Hard-surfaced "rugs" were designed to aid cleanup and to add a gay note of color to a 1929 kitchen. (Courtesy Congoleum Corporation.)

The one problem that remained unsolved was one recognized almost a century before—the servantless household. During World War II the matter could no longer be ignored; live-in household servants were gone forever. A maid, if available, would work on a daily basis and have the status of an office worker or factory worker. A partial solution to the problem became possible when electricity and mechanical power for household tasks and chores became available nationwide. Machines could take over some of the work previously done by individuals. Many still yearn for the "good old days." They forget that modern mechanization. mass production, and distribution make our standard of living the best in the world.

During World War II there were many advertisements and articles about the "kitchen of tomorrow." The kitchen of the 1930s had many laborsaving devices which had been developed and arranged in an efficient manner. Much of the household drudgery had been eliminated in the small, efficient kitchen, but it had isolated the housewife from her household.

The social changes, the servantless kitchen, and changes in attitudes produced the devel-

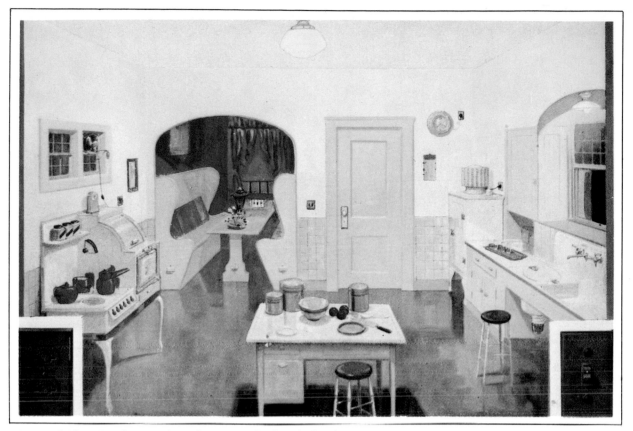

General Electric advocated modernizing the family kitchen with up-to-date wiring in 1930. Note swiveling fan which could be used for exhaust or for direct "breeze." (Courtesy General Electric Corporation.)

opment of a new design concept. It was simply not enough to have a food laboratory with perhaps a breakfast nook for informal meals. The postwar kitchen became larger, more open, and was intended to be an enjoyable room for work. The combination kitchen-dining room served as the center of family living. This concept eliminated the isolated room; however, general acceptance took a long time.

The meal preparation area remained an independent unit within the multipurpose room. It was efficient, stepsaving, and placed so that traffic did not pass through the work center. There was a large window, the desire of most women in the 1940s, for light and ventilation, which also made it possible to keep an eye on the children outside.

We have seen tremendous changes—from the large, dreary, unorganized room, to the sanitary kitchen where work was still drudgery, to a smaller kitchen with its touch of color —occuring in a period of twenty years. Spacesaving, timesaving arrangements were the next phase, and, finally, the colorful, streamlined kitchen emerged. We have many similar features, arrangements, and appliances in the "living" kitchens of the 1980s. The basic planning principles formulated and developed for the kitchen during the period from 1920 to 1950, remain fundamental, even in the microwave era.

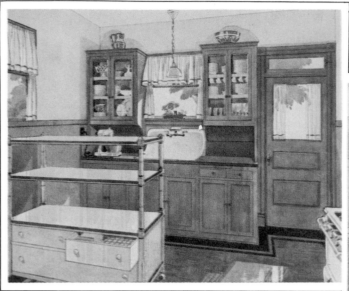

In 1932 *Household* magazine featured these kitchens designed by their planning staff. Wall-hung sinks were enclosed to form an unbroken unit with the base cabinets.

Looking surprisingly up-to-date by today's standards, this French Provincial kitchen was shown in a 1932 advertisement from the P & G Company.

Kitchen pictured in a 1933 magazine was considered very stylish with its color-coordinated cupboard unit and two-toned refrigerator. Isolated, wall-hung sink had no work surfaces around it. (Courtesy Congoleum Corporation.)

Four years later, in 1937, Congoleum floor covering was displayed in this large, streamlined kitchen. (Courtesy Congoleum Corporation.)

Comfortable breakfast nook of this 1940 kitchen was conveniently served from the L-shaped counter. (Courtesy Congoleum Corporation.)

Small eating area and built-in sink were attractive innovations in a kitchen pictured in a 1939 magazine. (Courtesy Armstrong Cork Company.)

Although World War II had not ended in 1944, homemakers and manufacturers of kitchen equipment were not to be caught with their plans down. This postwar kitchen included a dishwasher, garbage disposer, and a family-sized refrigerator with small freezer. These products did not become generally available for several years after the end of the war. (Courtesy General Electric—Hotpoint.)

"Maidless kitchen" advertisement from 1943 publication featured a sliding-door cabinet for "hiding dirty dishes underneath the sink," and a wheel-about serving-dining table. (Courtesy Armstrong Cork Company.)

Accessories in color.

Where do we go from here?

Accessories in Color

When kitchen equipment and accessories were introduced in colors, they proved to be an overwhelming success. The colors were attractive, cheerful, and certainly a welcome addition for the coordinated kitchen.

Author's collection.

If colored utensils were desired, enamelware, with its large variety of pieces, was available in the most alluring shades of green, yellow, tangerine, red, or blue. It also could be purchased with contrasting color trim.

Matching canisters, breadboxes, cake savers, match holders, salt and pepper shakers, and spice sets were offered individually. Cookie boxes, bread boards, knife boxes, towel racks, recipe boxes, step stools, clocks, trays, and jars were part of the vast array.

Colorful waste cans, dustpans, vegetable bins, waxed paper and towel dispensers, and garbage cans in enameled metal were also available.

These accessories were sometimes decorated with flowers or figures for an added touch of interest. Housewives were pleased to have these useful and decorative items because they were bright and made the kitchen picturesque and friendly.

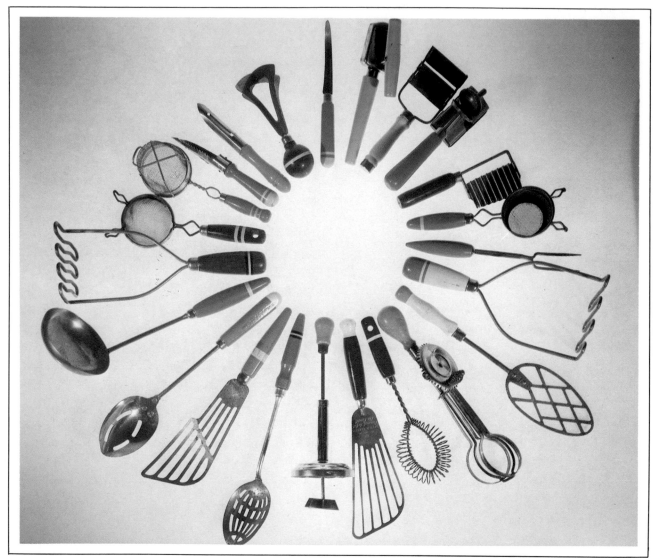

Handle potpourri.

18. The 1940s kitchen was streamlined. Note the slanted sink splashback.

17. Advertisement for custom-made Kitchen-Maid cabinets appeared in 1939.

19. Hotpoint ran this ad in 1942, but wartime restrictions made this a kitchen to dream about.

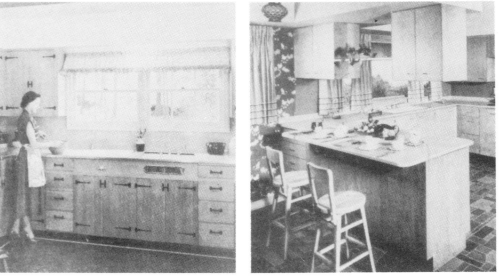

20. Kitchens in 1952 were large and efficient.

21. Plenty of sunlight, a modular range, wooden cabinets accented with brick made this 1952 kitchen charming and convenient.

Manufacturers from A to Z

Over the years, there have been numerous manufacturers of kitchen tools and gadgets. This alphabetical listing highlights many of the major manufacturers in the 1920s, 1930s, and 1940s.* You'll also find dozens of smaller companies. Some of these have since merged with the larger ones, and some have gone out of business. Many of the smaller companies will be cross-referenced under the larger corporations that acquired them.

A & J MANUFACTURING COMPANY, Binghamton, New York. The company was started in 1909 by Benjamin T. Ash and Edward H. Johnson with Johnson's purchase of a patent for an improved egg beater (mechanically operated with an up-and-down motion like a top). The business originally was located behind the Johnson home, and Johnson became sole owner in 1919.

The company made kitchen tools with natural wooden handles before producing colored handled tools. The first color was black, made about 1914; the second was white, made about 1916. About 1925, A & J introduced other colors: green, red, blue, and yellow. A common problem A & J shared with other manufacturers was with the enamel used which would peel, wear, or crack. The company tested many enamel samples to see which could withstand washing. In 1927, after many vigorous tests, Pittsburgh Plate Glass enamel was chosen and used continuously by them until enameled handles were discontinued on kitchen tools and gadgets.

A & J had a large domestic business and exported to Europe and South America. The company sold directly to chain stores, mail order houses, department stores, and major hardware jobbers. The largest chain store customer was F. W. Woolworth Company. Other chains included G. C. Murphy, Kress, Kresge, and the McCrory companies. Sears,

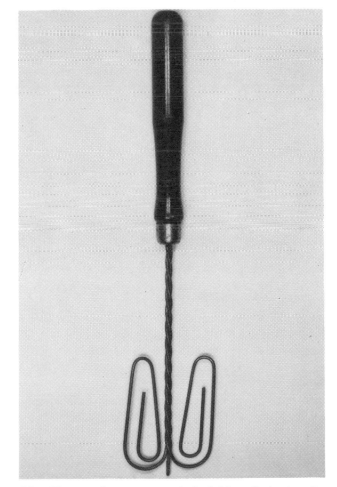

22. This eggbeater gave A & J Manufacturing its start. (Courtesy of Kenneth E. Johnson.)

*Information obtained from *A Buying Guide/Household Products* tested and approved by Good Housekeeping Institute, May 15, 1941.

Roebuck, Montgomery Ward, and Spiegel were also customers. A better line, made with stainless steel, was sold to major independent department stores across the country. Kitchen items were also used as promotional giveaways to new subscribers of newspapers and new customers for ice companies. Baking powder and flour companies such as Calumet, Rumford, Gold Medal, and Pillsbury used them as premiums. Even an undertaker in Iowa once gave away a kitchen tool set with each funeral.

By 1929, A & J had become the largest producer of kitchen tools. On February 8 of that year, Johnson told the Tri-City Industrial Club of Binghamton, New York, how his firm with more than 200 employees made up to 4 million kitchen tools a year.

The Edward Katzinger Company bought this successful enterprise in October, 1929, and in 1931 the company was moved to Chicago. (See EKCO Housewares Company.)

ACE MANUFACTURING CORPORATION, Philadelphia, Pennsylvania. This company made knife sharpeners, SERVA-SPOONs™, and potato creamers. By 1941, the name had been changed to Ace Hardware Manufacturing Corporation and was located at 2020 East Orleans Street, Philadelphia, Pennsylvania.*

ACME METAL GOODS MANUFACTURING COMPANY, Newark, New Jersey. The company, founded in 1900 by August C. Fischer, manufactures household hardware and specialities in metal, wire, and wood. From the beginning, Acme made kitchen tools and gadgets. Acme used natural and black wooden handles in the 1920s. Green, blue, red, and yellow enameled handles were introduced in the 1930s. Green and blue handles were the most popular. Kitchen items included garnishing sets, rotary mincers, potato peelers, food graters, egg slicers, kitchen tongs, ice picks, single and double blade food choppers, and grapefruit corers. The products were sold to wholesalers and to major chains such as F. W. Woolworth.

The Acme Company wrote the spiels about its products which firms giving product demonstrations used. Such demonstrations were given in places that attracted a large number of people, such as the boardwalk in Atlantic City, New Jersey, housewares shows, and fairs. This family-owned concern continues to manufacture modern versions of many of its earlier products.

ALUMINUM GOODS MANUFACTURING COMPANY, Two Rivers, Wisconsin. Joseph Koenig started the company in 1895. It merged with two other companies to become the Aluminum Goods Manufacturing Company in 1908. The MIRRO™ brand name has been used since 1917. In 1957 the corporate name was changed to Mirro Aluminum Company of Manitowac, Wisconsin. Recently, in 1979, the stockholders voted to adopt Mirro Corporation as the company name.

AMERICAN CUTTER COMPANY, Milwaukee, Wisconsin. This firm manufactured Roll-Em-Out™ doughnut cutters, Roll-Em-Out™ molasses cookie cutters, and Roll-Em-Out™ tea wafer cutters.

ANDREWS WIRE and IRON WORKS, Rockford, Illinois. Founded by Charles Andrews in 1885, the company prospered and expanded in 1910 by setting up a Canadian division in Watford, Ontario. The subsidiary was called the Andrews Wire Works of Canada Limited. The trademark used was ANDROCK, which referred to Andrews and Rockford. The Andrews Wire and Iron Works joined forces with the Washburn Company of Worcester, Massachusetts in 1917. (See Washburn Company.)

APEX PRODUCTS CORPORATION, New York City, New York. It manufactured the Chip-Chop™ ice pick.

BAL-SO. This name appears on a child's eggbeater.

BROMWELL WIRE GOODS, Cincinnati, Ohio. Founded by Jacob Bromwell in 1819, the company is the oldest housewares firm continuously in business. It is now the Bromwell Products Division of Leigh Products, Inc., of Michigan City, Indiana. The products were sold primarily in five-and-dime stores, mail order houses, and hardware stores. The firm still produces rotary cranks, shakers, and squeeze-type sifters with metal handles and wooden knobs.

CARBORUNDUM COMPANY, Niagara Falls, New York. This company made octagonal knife sharpeners, knife sharpeners for stainless steel, and household stones. It became a subsidiary of Kennecott Copper Corporation, December 31, 1977.

E. W. CARPENTER MANUFACTURING COMPANY, 1565 Railroad Avenue, Bridgeport, Connecticut, manufactured EVER-SHARP™ knife sharpeners.*

CENTRAL STATES MANUFACTURING COMPANY, St. Louis, Missouri. This firm manufactured SPEEDO SUPER JUICERS™. When it was acquired by Dazey Churn and Manufacturing Company, the juicer became the DAZEY SPEEDO SUPER JUICER™. (See Dazey Churn and Manufacturing Company.)

CHICAGO DIE CASTING MANUFAC-TURING COMPANY, Chicago, Illinois. This firm made ORANGE FLOW™ juicers.

CHICAGO PRECISION PRODUCTS CORPORATION, Chicago, Illinois. This firm made an ice chopper and glass jar combination (a turbine beater and glass bowl). A present day company with the same name never made these products. (It manufactures screw machine products.)

CLYDE CUTLERY COMPANY, Clyde, Ohio. This company was established by Hunter and Brigham in 1869 and continued until July 25, 1970, when the factory burned to the ground. It produced various cutlery including bread knives and pastry sets.

COLUMBIA. Brand name of a family scales made by Landers, Frary, and Clark. (See Landers, Frary, and Clark.)

CONTINENTAL GEM COMPANY. This firm made tea strainers.

CONTINENTAL SCALES WORKS, Chicago, Illinois. This company was founded by Mathias C. Weber and Alfred and Irving Hutchison on January 17, 1919.

CRITERION. This name appears on a child's eggbeater.

DAZEY CHURN and MANUFACTURING COMPANY, 4315 Warne Avenue, St. Louis, Missouri.* Some of its products were fruit juice extractors, ice crushers, knife sharpeners, can openers, and churns. It acquired Central States Manufacturing Company who manufac-tured SPEEDO SUPER JUICERS™ in the 1930s. The name was changed to the DAZEY CORPORATION, and in 1945, it became a subsidiary of Landers, Frary, and Clark.

DOMINION ELECTRICAL MANUFAC-TURING COMPANY, Minneapolis, Minne-sota. It manufactured electrical appliances such as corn poppers and waffle irons. The company became known as the Dominion Elec-trical Corporation and was acquired in April, 1969, by Scovill Manufacturing Company. Currently, it is part of the Hamilton-Beach Divi-sion of Scovill, Inc.

DUPLEX-WHIPPER CORPORATION, Chicago, Illinois. It made Duplex Cream & Egg Whippers.

DURABILT. This name appears on a grapefruit corer.

DURO METAL PRODUCTS, 2449 North Kildare Avenue, Chicago, Illinois.* This firm manufactured WHIPPET™ cream and egg whips and SKIMIT™ cream skimmers.

EDLUND COMPANY, INC., Burlington, Vermont. This company was founded by Henry J. Edlund who invented an institutional can opener in 1925. Its success prompted his design of a household version, the EDLUND JUNIOR #5™, which was patented in 1927. He also invented and had patented the EDLUND egg beater, TOP-OFF™ (a device to remove screw tops from jars and bottles), and SURE SHARP™ (a knife sharpener). The company's kitchen utensil line was sold to the Bonny Prod-ucts Company of Hewlett, New York, in 1973. Modern versions, with plastic handles, of the EDLUND JUNIOR #5™ can opener and TOP-OFF™ jar opener are still available today. These items are sold through distributors who sell to retail stores.

EKCO HOUSEWARES COMPANY, Chi-cago, Illinois. The Edward Katzinger Company was founded in 1888 to produce commercial baking pans. In 1923, it began to manufacture a line of bread and cake pans for home use. EKCO, the company trademark, was derived from the founder's initials. Its first acquisition was in 1927 with the purchase of the August Maag Company of Baltimore, Maryland, a small commercial bakeware manufacturer. EKCO entered the kitchen tool business when it acquired the A & J Manufacturing Company of Binghamton, New York, in 1929. The plant in Binghamton was closed in 1931, and the opera-tion was moved to Chicago. In 1930, the com-pany featured NUKOLOR™ handles, "an exclu-sive A & J Innovation to meet the New Vogue in Colorful Kitchen Decoration." The NUKOLOR™ handles offered a great variety of color combi-nations in stripes or bands and tips.

EKCO continued its policy of purchasing profitable companies. In 1934, it acquired the

Geneva Cutlery Company of Geneva, New York, and continued to market the cutlery under the Geneva Forge trademark. The Sta-Brite Products Corporation, New Haven, Connecticut, manufacturers of stainless steel flatware, was purchased in 1943. This company is generally credited with introducing Catalin, one of the first plastics to be used for cutlery handles.

The E. L. Tebbets Spool Company, Inc., of Locke Mills, Maine, was acquired in 1945. Prior to World War I, it almost exclusively manufactured wooden spools for thread. After the war, it began to diversify and to manufacture handles for kitchen utensils, hand tools, and a wide variety of novel turnings. This company has made handles continuously for A & J and has manufactured handles for Androck, Edlund, and Foley. The company is now known as Ekco Wood Products Company.

EKCO went into wartime production during World War II, making machine gun bullet clips and brass shell casings. The company was allowed to manufacture a limited number of kitchen utensils. The production of the MIRACLE™ can opener never ceased, because it was considered an essential item. EKCO's number one selling item continues to be the MIRACLE™ can opener.

Corporate expansions through the years have made EKCO the largest producer of non-electric housewares. The name of the company was changed to EKCO Products Company in 1945. The EKCO Housewares Company, as it is now known, became a division of the American Home Products Company in 1965. It produces more than 3,500 houseware items today, many of which are modern versions of the kitchen tools and gadgets from the 1920s to the 1940s.

ELECTRAHOT MANUFACTURING COMPANY, Minneapolis, Minnesota. It produced electric toasters.

ENTERPRISE ALUMINUM COMPANY, Massillon, Ohio. It manufactured DRIP-O-LATOR™ coffeepots and other aluminum cookware. The company, acquired by Lancaster Colony Corporation, is now located in Macon, Georgia, and continues to manufacture aluminum cookware.

FEDERAL TOOL CORPORATION, Chicago, Illinois. This firm made nut choppers, pitchers, and syrup jars.

FOLEY MANUFACTURING COMPANY, Minneapolis, Minnesota. Founded by Walter Ringer in 1926, the company entered the kitchen utensil business in 1933 with the purchase of a French patent for a device to become known as the FOLEY FOOD MILL™. In spite of the Depression, the food mill became a success because it proved to be a money saver for the homemaker and a canning device without equal.

During World War II the firm's defense production included mess kits, canteen cups, duffle bags, and canteen covers. This family-owned company, with its diversified holdings, is a leading manufacturer of kitchen tools and gadgets and produces such items as the food mill, chopper, mixing fork, and trigger action (SIFT-CHINE™ type) sifters. (See Meets-A-Need Manufacturing Corporation.)

GADGET MANUFACTURING COMPANY, Los Angeles, California. The three-blade lifter was one of its products.

GENEVA CUTLERY COMPANY, Geneva, New York. (See EKCO Housewares Company.)

GENUINE. This was the name on a rotary sifter.

GRIP-ALL. The name was on a screw cap jar opener.

HAMILTON METAL PRODUCTS COMPANY, Hamilton, Ohio. CLIMAX™ rotary graters were made by this concern.*

HANDY ANDY SPECIALTY COMPANY, INC., 30–40 22nd Street, Long Island City, New York, in 1931. It was located at 534 Van Alst Avenue, Long Island City, New York, in 1941.* It manufactured juice extractors and knife sharpeners.

HANDY THINGS, Houghton, Michigan. This company produced food presses.

D. HARRINGTON and SONS, Southbridge, Massachusetts. Paring knives were possibly manufactured by Harrington Cutlery.

HAZEL-ATLAS GLASS COMPANY, Wheeling, West Virginia. In 1886 C. N. Brady started the Hazel Glass Company in Wellsburg, West Virginia. The company merged with the Atlas Glass Company of Washington, Pennsylvania, in 1902 to become known as the Hazel-Atlas Glass Company. However, the H over A trademark was not used until the 1920s. Hazel-Atlas made the glass for A & J beater and bowl and pitcher sets from 1924 until those items were discontinued in 1959. By the 1950s, company operations had grown to thirteen factories with thirty-three furnaces. It had become a leading manufacturer of wide mouth containers of all kinds. Continental Can Company took it over in 1958 and continued operations until 1964.

HI-SPEED. This name was on a grapefruit corer.

HOUSEHOLD SPECIALTIES. This name was on an ice pick.

IDEAL PRODUCTS COMPANY, Brooklyn, New York. It manufactured AID-U-HANDY™ tools.

EDWARD KATZINGER COMPANY. (See A & J Manufacturing Company and EKCO Housewares Company).

KITCHENEED PRODUCTS COMPANY, Buffalo, New York; Fort Erie, Canada. It was listed in the Buffalo telephone directory only in 1934, 1935, and 1936, with Melvin R. Henry, manager house furnishings, at 36 West Huron Street. The company manufactured kitchen knife sets. In 1941, Good Housekeeping Institute approved KITCHENEED™ ring garnisher, the garnishing set, and food mincer manufactured by Manufacturers Specialties Company, 1252 Voskamp Street, Pittsburgh, Pennsylvania.

KITCHEN NOVELTY MANUFACTURERS COMPANY, Atlantic City, New Jersey. This company made grapefruit corers.

KRISTEE PRODUCTS COMPANY, Akron, Ohio. This household specialty company was established in 1925 by Wm. C. Krisher. The first household product was a waterproof apron of percale or print cloth which was specially treated with a rubber backing. Kristee Products always had between 75 and 100 different items in its catalog. Some of these were manufactured or assembled by the company; others were purchased and labeled with Kristee's name. The meat tenderizers with colored handles were available from 1935 to 1950. The products are still sold nationwide by door-to-door independent salesmen.

KWIKWAY PRODUCTS COMPANY, St. Louis, Missouri. This company made juice extractors.

LANDERS, FRARY, and CLARK, New Britain, Connecticut. In 1882 the Landers and Smith Company acquired the firm of Frary and Clark of New Britain, Connecticut, one of the best known manufacturers of housewares and hardware. In the 1890s, the trade name "Universal" was adopted and put on a variety of products. Included in the kitchenware line were scales, percolators, can openers, cutlery, toasters, and juicers. In 1965, the company was acquired by General Electric's housewares division.

LORRAINE METAL COMPANY, New York City, New York. This company manufactured rotary and spring action choppers.

MANUFACTURED SPECIALTIES COMPANY, 1252 Voskamp Street, Pittsburgh, Pennsylvania.* Its products included KITCHENEED™ ring garnishers, KITCHENEED™ garnishing sets, and KITCHENEED™ food mincers.

JOSEPH A. MARTOCELLO and COMPANY, 229–231 North 13th Street, Philadelphia, Pennsylvania.* The company made CHIP-CHOP™ and DU-MORE™ ice cubers.

MEETS-A-NEED MANUFACTURING COMPANY, 2955 Utah Street, Seattle, Washington. The company was owned by Donald Dickey who employed handicapped persons to make SIFT-CHINE™ flour sifters. In the late 1940s, it was acquired by the Foley Manufacturing Company. Today the company still employs handicapped persons who make the same sifters. (See Foley Manufacturing Company.)

FRED J. MEYERS MANUFACTURING COMPANY, Hamilton, Ohio. This company manufactured HUNTER™ flour sifters.

MIRACLE GEM. This name was on a tea strainer.

MIRACLE PRODUCTS INC., Chicago, Illinois. The company made electric flour sifters.

M P., Los Angeles, California. This trademark was on an egg boiler.

M S Co. A bottle and jar opener bore this trade name.

NATIONAL ENAMELING and STAMPING COMPANY, 213 North 12th Street, Milwaukee, Wisconsin.* The company was founded in 1899 and manufactured a variety of products, including NESCO™ sifters, funnel-strainers, and ACME™ sifters. NESCO became the trade name in the 1930s. In 1955 the company merged with the Knapp-Monarch Company of St. Louis, and in 1969 it became part of the Knapp-Monarch Division of the Hoover Company. Products under the NESCO name are still manufactured.

NATIONAL STAMPING and ELECTRIC WORKS, 3212 West Lake Street, Chicago, Illinois.* This firm made WHITE CROSS™ waffle irons, coffee makers, and hot plates.

NEW STANDARD CORPORATION, Pinkerton Road, Mount Joy, Pennsylvania.* This company made rotary food choppers and DANDY™ cherry stoners in the 1920s and 1930s. It is still in business.

NORTON COMPANY, Worcester, Massachusetts. Established in 1885, the company made knife sharpeners in the 1930s and continues to manufacture a wide range of abrasives. With corporate growth, it is now known as Norton, Inc..

OCKO. This name appeared on an orange peeler.

PARAGON. A flour sifter showed this name.

P M COMPANY. Kitchen tools were manufactured by this firm.

PRESTO. This name appeared on a knife sharpener.

"PRESTO." A jar lifter had this name on it.

QUIKUT, INC., Fremont, Ohio. The company was started as Close-Witcomb in January, 1920 in Clyde, Ohio. In July, 1920, the name was changed to Clyde Castings Company. The company made paring knives and a can opener in the latter part of 1921. L. K. Carroll purchased the company, moving it to Fremont, Ohio. In 1936 its largest order was for 500,000 paring knives to be given as premiums by the W. A. Rawleigh Company, a door-to-door sales company of household products such as vanilla and allspice. Colored wooden handles were used prior to 1950. The company name was changed to Quikut, Inc., in 1948, the trade name used on the cutlery. The company became a division of Scott and Fetter Company on November 30, 1964. Today it continues to make kitchen cutlery.

RAPID. This name appears on a dough blender.

REMARK MANUFACTURING COMPANY, Butler, Indiana. This company made vegetable slicers and shredders under the SIMPLEX trade name.

RIVAL MANUFACTURING COMPANY, Kansas City, Missouri. Henry Talge established this company in 1932. Rival was one of the early producers of manual juicers. Other appliances it manufactured in the early 1930s were a bean slicer/pea sheller, a manually operated can opener, a JUICE-O-MAT™, and a JAR-O-MAT™ for opening jars. The firm is still in operation.

ROBERTS. This was the name on an ice cream scoop.

ROTARY. A knife sharpener showed this name.

RUMFORD CHEMICAL WORKS, Rumford, Rhode Island. Rumford offered cooking utensils as premiums during various years from 1900 to 1930. The dates and the manufacturers of these premiums are not available. The company came under its present ownership in 1950. The office and plant were moved to Terre Haute, Indiana, in 1966.

SAFE-T-MANUFACTURING COMPANY, Chicago, Illinois. This company manufactured can openers.

SAMSON CUTLERY COMPANY, Rochester, New York. The company was established by Abe O. Samson. Although it was listed only in the 1924 and 1925 Rochester city directory, Earl Lifshey in the *Housewares Story* said that in 1929 Samson Cutlery Company of Rochester, New York, introduced "waterproof and crack-proof handles" on a line of stainless steel kitchen tools.

SAVORY, INC., 591 Ferry Street, Newark, New Jersey.* It made SAVORY JUNIOR™ flour sifters.

SCHACHT RUBBER COMPANY, Huntington, Indiana. This company manufactured DAISY™ rubber spatulas, scrapers, and sink plungers. Family-owned, the company is still in business.

SELECT SPTS. COMPANY, New York City, New York. This company made SURE-HOLD™ utensil cleaners.

STEELCRAFT. A mechanical beater bore this name.

STOMAR, Philadelphia, Pennsylvania. This company made grapefruit corers.

SWING-A-WAY MANUFACTURING COMPANY, St. Louis, Missouri. Formerly the Steel Products Manufacturing Company, it was renamed Swing-A-Way Manufacturing Company in 1948. It still manufactures can openers.

THE TAPLIN MANUFACTURING COMPANY, New Britain, Connecticut. The first listing for this company appeared in the New Britain city directory in 1901 with Fred Goodrich as president and treasurer. It was listed in Good Housekeeping Institute's *Buyer's Guide* in 1941. The company made can openers and eggbeaters.

TAYLOR INSTRUMENT COMPANIES, Rochester, New York. This company made household thermometers in the 1930s and continues to do so today. It is now a division of the Sybron Corporation.

TODDY. This name appears on a drink mixer.

TURNER AND SEYMOUR MANUFACTURING COMPANY, Torrington, Connecticut. BLUE WHIRL™, MERRY WHIRL™, and T & S™ eggbeaters, BLUE STREAK™ grapefruit corers, pea shellers, and can opening machines were made by this company.

TYLER MANUFACTURING COMPANY, Muncie, Indiana. This company manufactured meat tenderizer-axes.

UNEEK UTILITIES CORPORATION, Chicago, Illinois. DUPLEX™ sifter was manufactured by this company.

UNITED ROYALTIES CORPORATION, 1133 Broadway, New York City, New York.* This company made various LADD™ eggbeaters.

U.S. MANUFACTURING CORPORATION, Decatur, Illinois.* This company manufactured non-electric corn poppers.

VAUGHAN NOVELTY MANUFACTURING COMPANY, 3211 Carroll Avenue, Chicago, Illinois.* Pie trimmers and sealers and apple corers were among the products this company manufactured.

VIDRIO PRODUCTS CORPORATION, Chicago, Illinois. This company made electric cream whippers.

VILLA. A french fry cutter bore this name.

WALLACE BROTHERS, Connecticut. This company probably manufactured kitchen tools with the WB over W trademark.

THE WASHBURN COMPANY, Worcester, Massachusetts. In 1880, Charles G. Washburn established the company in Boston and, in November of that year, moved it to Worcester, Massachusetts. The business was incorporated under the name of Wire Goods Company in 1882.

Its western division, Wire Hardware Company, was established in 1911 in Chicago. The well-established firm of Cassady-Fairbank Manufacturing Company of Chicago was purchased in 1914. Three years later, the Wire Goods Company (Worcester, Massachusetts) merged with the Andrews Wire and Iron Works, Rockford, Illinois, and its Canadian subsidiary. (See Andrews Wire and Iron Works.) The merger of these two companies with similar interests and four separate firms, became known as Associated Companies.

In 1918, the Wire Hardware Company was dissolved and the western operations consolidated under the name of Cassady-Fairbank Manufacturing Company of Chicago. The three American companies (the Wire Goods Company of Worcester, the Cassady-Fairbank Company of Chicago, and the Andrews Wire and Iron Works of Rockford) were consolidated under one name, the Washburn Company, in 1922. The Canadian Company and the Michigan Wire Goods Company of Niles, Michigan (acquired in 1923), operated as separate companies under the Washburn policy. The Chicago division was closed, and operations were continued by the Rockford and Worcester plants in 1929.

In the early twenties, the Washburn Company was among the first houseware manufacturers to bring color to the kitchen with its lacquered wooden handles on kitchen tools. The entire ANDROCK™ line was redesigned in 1934 with the introduction of Androck Balanced Kitchenware and its "Handle That Fits the Hand." The tools were available in red, yellow, green, and banded green with a teardrop handle. The company continued to use this style handle until the early 1940s.

The Washburn Company completely withdrew from its civilian business during World War II to devote its entire production to the war effort. It manufactured a variety of parts for tanks, weapons, and planes; tent hardware, field kitchen utensils, bomb racks, and many more items.

Roblin Steel Corporation of Buffalo, New York, acquired the Washburn Company in 1967, and the name was changed to Androck Company. Roblin closed the Rockford, Illinois, factory and moved all operations to the Worcester, Massachusetts, plant in 1973.

In 1965 the name Andrew Wire Works of Canada Limited was changed to Androck Limited, and in 1974, it was sold separately to Canadian interests. The present company, Androck, Inc., of Watford, Ontario, holds the sole rights to the Androck name and trademark in Canada.

The plant and equipment of the Androck Company of Worcester, Massachusetts, were sold at auction in 1975. Various American firms purchased the equipment and still manufacture some Androck products, all using the same Androck trademark (Androck in an oval), because it is part of the tooling purchased. The offering of Androck products by competing companies has proved confusing.

WHIPWELL. This name appeared on an eggbeater.

WIZARD. There were grapefruit corers manufactured with this trademark.

WOLVERINE TOY, Booneville, Arkansas. This company, still in Booneville, is now a subsidiary of Spang Industries, Inc. It made Sunny Suzy™ children's toy irons.

YATES MANUFACTURING COMPANY, Chicago, Illinois. Parer slicers were made by this company.

YO-HO. A jar lifter bore this name.

ZIM MANUFACTURING COMPANY, Chicago, Illinois. This company made wall mounted can openers.

A Guide to Trademarks

A trademark identifies and distinguishes the products of one company from another. It may consist of a word, sentence, name, symbol, picture, or any combination of these. The spoken part of the trademark is called a brand name. Brand names reflect the reputation of a company. They are marketing symbols used by manufacturers to promote their goods by easy identification.

Laws were developed in the early 1800s to protect the rights of the trademark owner. Legally, the first person to use a trademark on the market has the right to that mark. However, unless it has been registered with the United States Patent and Trademark Office, others can use the same trademark on other unrelated products. Since 1905 it has been possible to make application to register a trademark. Once officially registered, the owner is guaranteed the right to exclusive use of the trademark for twenty years, a right that is renewable and transferrable.

The trademark symbol is often used on unregistered marks to indicate a common law claim of rights. After a trademark is registered in the United States Patent and Trademark Office an ® or "Reg. U.S. Pat. & T.M. Off." may be used.

Following is a list of trademarks and tools they were used on. The registration date is in parentheses.

A & J Manufacturing Company — Edward Katzinger Company EKCO Housewares Company

(registered 1922)
kitchen tools

(registered 1925)
Used on goods or packages.

MOTHER'S LITTLE HELPER

(registered 1927)
Kits of juvenile kitchen utensils

(1932 version)
The A & J in a diamond trademark
was used until 1946.

(1937 version)

(1947 version)

EKCO

U.S.A.

(version after 1947)

Ace Manufacturing Corporation

knife sharpener

National Enameling and Stamping Company

ACME

flour sifter

Acme Metal Goods Manufacturing Company

choppers, mincers, graters

Ideal Products Company

AID-U-Handy Tool

icepick

The Washburn Company

Androck

(oldest trademark)
kitchen tools

(1946)
nut chopper

Androck

ANDROCK

(1934 to 1941)
balanced kitchenware

(1968)

44

Unknown Company

child's eggbeater

Rival Manufacturing Company

Can-O-Mat

can opener

Bromwell Wire Goods Company

Bromwell

XXX flour sifter
(oldest trademark shown)

Carborundum Company

CARBORUNDUM

knife sharpener

BROMWELL'S

rotary flour sifter

rotary flour sifter

BROMWELL'S
DUET

horizontal sifter

Chicago Precision Products Corporation

CHICAGO
PRECISION PRODUCTS CORP.
CHICAGO. ILLS
PAT. APLD.

ice chopper, turbine beater and bowl

horizontal sifter

Apex Products Corporation

icepick

Hamilton Metal Products Company

★ ★ CLIMAX ★ ★

rotary grater

Continental Gem Company

"CONT'L. GEM CO."
"MADE IN U.S.A."

tea strainer

Clyde Cutlery Company

bread knife

Criterion

CRITERION

child's eggbeater

bread knife

Schacht Rubber Manufacturing Company

DAISY

rubber spatula, plate scraper

Landers, Frary and Clark

COLUMBIA

household scale

New Standard Corporation

De LUXE

NEW STANDARD CORP.

food chopper

Dominion Electrical Manufacturing Company

DEPENDABLE DOMINO DEVICES

electric corn popper

Continental Scale Works

Continental Scale Works

household scale

Enterprise Aluminum Company

Drip-O-lator

coffeepot

Duplex-Whipper Corporation

turbine eggbeater

Uneek Utilities Corporation

DUPLEX SIFTER

flour sifter

Unknown Company

DURABILT GRAPE FRUIT CORER

Edlund Company, Inc.

EDLUND CO.

beater, jar opener, can opener

Edlund

later model can opener

Ekco Housewares Company

(registered 1917)
kitchen tools

(registered 1946)
kitchen tools

EKCO

mechanical eggbeater

(registered 1959)
kitchen tools

EKCO ETERNA

apple corer

(registered 1963)
kitchen tools

Electrahot Manufacturing Company

ELECTRAHOT MFG.CO

toaster

E. W. Carpenter Manufacturing Company

Eversharp

knife sharpener

Federal Tool Corporation

nut chopper

FEDERAL TOOL CORP.

nut chopper

Foley Manufacturing Company

FOLEY

food mill, chopper

Foley

flour sifter

EKCO Housewares Company

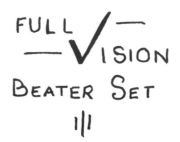

FULL ✓—
—✓ISION
BEATER SET
I|I

beater and metal bowl set

Gadget Manufacturing Company

GADGET MFG.

three-blade lifter

Geneva Cutlery Company

later trademark

Geneva Stainless U.S.A.

grapefruit knife

Unknown Company

GENUINE

flour sifter

Unknown Company

"GRIP-ALL"

jar opener

Turner and Seymour Manufacturing Company

HANDIMAID

glass pitcher from beater set

Handy Andy Specialty Company, Inc.

HANDY ANDY

juicer

Handy Things

food press

D. Harrington and Son

D. HARRINGTON & SON

paring knife

Hazel-Atlas

glass pitcher from beater set,
nut chopper

A & J Manufacturing Company
EKCO Housewares Company

HIGH SPEED

eggbeater

eggbeater, later version

Unknown Company

grapefruit corer

Household Specialties

icepick

Fred J. Meyers Manufacturing Company

HUNTER'S SIFTER.
STANDARD OF THE WORLD

flour sifter

Rival Manufacturing Company

Juice-O-Mat

juicer

EKCO Housewares Company

Kitchamajig

Kitchen Novelty Company

KITCHEN NOVELTY Co.

grapefruit corer

Kristee Products Company

meat tenderizer

Kwikway Products Company

KWIKWAY

juicer

United Royalties Corporation

LADD

early eggbeater

LADD BEATER

eggbeater

Lorraine Metal Manufacturing Company

LORRAINE METAL

MFG CO

rotary chopper, rotary grater

Joseph A. Martocello and Company

MARTOCELLO

icepick

Turner and Seymour Manufacturing Company

MERRY
WHIRL

eggbeater and lid

EKCO Housewares Company

MIRACLE

can opener

Miracle Products, Inc.

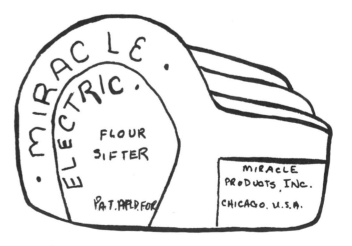

flour sifter

Miracle Gem

MIRACLE GEM

tea strainer

Norton Company

knife sharpener

Fred J. Meyers Manufacturing Company

THE FRED. J. MEYERS M'F'G CO.

flour sifter

Unknown Company

OCKO

orange peeler

Unknown Company

egg boiler

Chicago Die Manufacturing Company

juicer

M S Company

bottle opener

Unknown Company

PARAGON

flour sifter

National Enameling and Stamping Company

sifter, funnel-strainer

Kitchen Novelty Company

THE PERFECT CORER

grapefruit corer

P M Company

slotted spoon

Unknown Company

PRESTO

knife sharpener

Unknown Company

jar lifter

Norton Company

QUICKCUT

knife sharpener

Quikut, Inc.

paring knife

Unknown Company

dough blender

Unknown Company

ROBERTS

ice cream scoop

American Cutter Company

revolving cookie cutter

Unknown Company

knife sharpener

Safe-T-Manufacturing Company

can opener

Samson Cutlery Company

kitchen tools

bread knife

Unknown Company

flour sifter

Unknown Company

SHARP - EZY

knife sharpener

Meets-A-Need Manufacturing Company

SIFT - CHINE

flour sifter

Remark Manufacturing Company

SIMPLEX

vegetable slicer

Central States Manufacturing Company

juicer

A & J Manufacturing Company

SPINNIT

turbine beater

Unknown Company

STEELCRAFT

mechanical beater

Unknown Company

grapefruit corer

Wolverine Toy

child's iron

53

Select Spts. Company

SUREHOLD

utensil cleaner

Edlund Company, Inc.

SURE SHARP

knife sharpener

Swing-A-Way Manufacturing Company

Swing-A-Way

can opener

Turner and Seymour Manufacturing Company

T & S

beater and bowl set

The Taplin Manufacturing Company

Betty Taplin (EGG) Beater

child's eggbeater

The Taplin Manufacturing Company

eggbeater

Taylor Instrument Companies

Taylor

thermometer

Rival Manufacturing Company

" TILT TOP "

juicer

Unknown Company

drink mixer

Edlund Company, Inc.

jar opener

Landers, Frary, and Clark

juicer

Vidrio Products Corporation

electric beater

United States Manufacturing Corporation

corn popper

Unknown Company

THE
"VILLA"
POTATO
CHIPPER

french fry cutter

The Washburn Company

eggbeater

Vaughan Novelty Manufacturing Company

apple corer

Wallace Brothers *(probably)*

WB
W

kitchen tools

Vaughan's

pie trimmer and sealer

Duro Metal Products Company

turbine beater

EKCO Housewares Company

turbine beater

(This was registered
in 1928 to White and
Hallock, Inc. and assigned to the
EKCO Housewares Company in 1945.)

Unknown Company

WHIPWELL

eggbeater

National Stamping and Electric Works

waffle iron

Unknown Company

grapefruit corer

Wolverine Toy

child's iron

Yates Manufacturing Company

YATES MFG. CO.
CHICAGO

vegetable parer

Unknown Company

YO-HO

jar lifter

Zim Manufacturing Company

Finding and Purchasing Kitchen Tools

As antique kitchen gadgets become less available, prices soar. Collectibles from the 1920s, 1930s, and 1940s are becoming more desirable. These tools and gadgets are fascinating and have great appeal as an important element of the nostalgic past.

Some people are buying kitchen gadgets with wooden handles because they are well made, durable (still usable after forty or fifty years), and less expensive than modern counterparts.

There are many places to look for these collectibles—garage, yard, attic, porch, house, estate, rummage, tag, and white elephant sales; thrift shops, Good Will and Salvation Army stores; flea markets, auctions, and antique shops.

The prices listed in this book serve only as a current guide for asking prices. The buyer is really the final judge. If it seems a fair price, buy it; if it seems out of line, don't. Keep searching and you may find another. Part of the fun of collecting is seeking out special items. If you "have to have it," then pay the price.

Prices will vary according to time of purchase, source, geographic location, availability, condition, and quality. Fads also have an important affect on prices. Marked or unique kitchenware items command a higher price than the unmarked or ordinary. Quality kitchen tools and gadgets, the type sold in department stores bear higher prices. Surprisingly, even kitchenware in poor condition is being marketed.

Any tool or gadget should be usable as well as decorative or fashionable. Here is a guide to help you determine condition and value of kitchenware items:

Excellent—Unused, like new. Colored handles show no sign of chipping, cracking, or wear; metal has no corrosion or deterioration.
Very good—Slight use, almost new.
Good—Used. Colored handles have small amount of chipping or cracking; metal is in good condition.
Fair—Usable but shows wear. Metal has some deterioration or corrosion.
Poor—Not usable. Little color left on handles; metal is rusted and bent.

To care for these kitchen gadgets, use caution. Do not soak in water or put in dishwasher. Wash, rinse, and dry thoroughly. Do not use harsh detergents.

Background, Color, and Dating Information

Enameled and lacquered wooden handled tools and gadgets are still available kitchen collectibles. They were manufactured by numerous companies, bought by businesses or jobbers (distributors), and sold through department stores, hardware stores, variety stores, catalog and mail order houses, and specialty shops. Generally, jobbers ordered solid colored handles; mail order houses and chain stores ordered multicolored handles. Some companies, e.g., Rumford, S & H, and Proctor & Gamble, purchased these items directly from manufacturers for use as giveaways or premiums.

Metal parts of the tools were tin, nickel, or chrome-plated; tool steel or stainless steel. Although stainless steel was patented in 1911, it was not used for kitchen utensils until 1921. Stainless steel saved housewives many hours of scouring to remove discoloration or rust. Chief alloy of stainless steel is chromium, which resists corrosion and rust.

Tool steel, a tough high carbon steel, is used for knives and kitchen implements such as can openers and choppers.

In the early 1920s, a few housewares manufacturers started to bring color to the kitchen when they put colored wooden handles on kitchen tools. This introduction of color was a revolutionary concept in kitchen tool design which brought a note of cheerfulness and appeal to the kitchen. This theory of product design has continued to the present. The first colored wooden handles were black, followed by white, and were used prior to and during the 1920s. It wasn't until the late 1920s and 1930s that green became the most popular (or the most manufactured and available today) colored handle. Red, blue, and yellow handles were also produced. After colored handles were accepted, it was only a short time before banded, striped, and two-toned handles were

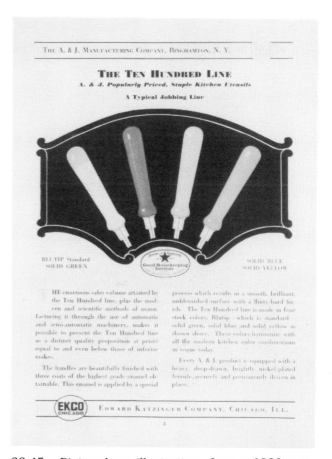

23-45. Pictured are illustrations from a 1930 catalog of the A & J Manufacturing Company. (Courtesy EKCO Housewares Company.)

made. The widespread use of red handles was evident in the late 1930s and 1940s. There were many complaints about the colored enameled and lacquered handles because the color rubbed, peeled, or chipped off.

The "Color in the Kitchen" promotion in 1927, launched by Macy's and Abraham & Strauss, featured color-coordinated kitchen tools, utensils, and accessories in apple green, mandarin red, and delft blue. There was a wide variation in these colors, with no two manufacturers' colors looking alike. This color problem stemmed from the fact there were no official or accepted color standards. It wasn't until 1938 that the U.S. Bureau of Standards developed official color standards for the kitchen which began to be adopted by the manufacturers.

In the late 1920s the term "gadget" came into use. Formerly, gadgets were known as household devices, kitchen novelties, kitchen specialities, or laborsaving devices. Americans have an inherent weakness for these creations of Yankee ingenuity—inexpensive devices that will save time, temper, and labor. They can be intriguing, appealing, ingenious, and many times so useful to some people that they become essential to perform a task.

Cookie cutters, strainers, can openers, ice picks, and other small kitchen items that stores found hard to display were kept in drawers. Sometime in the 1920s these gadgets were mounted on cards to display them in an attractive, eye-appealing manner which promoted impulse buying. Today, obtaining gadgets the way they were originally packaged is most informative. Many details are given on the card or package, such as the name, how to use the device, the manufacturer, possibly an address, and sometimes a date. The illustrations on the card or package are indicative of the era if the items are not dated. (In dating items, it is helpful to know that postal zoning was used from 1943 to 1963.)

Handles on tools from the A & J Manufacturing Company and Edward Katzinger Company (later known as the EKCO Housewares Company) were offered in a variety of colors from 1930 to 1949.

1930 catalog—bluetip, solid green, solid blue, and solid yellow.

1935 catalog—solid green, green with ivory band.

1936 catalog—green with ivory band and red with ivory band. White with green, red, blue, or black bands; lemon yellow with black band; or solid lemon yellow made on order. Any other color combination available on special order.

1937 catalog—solid green, solid delphinium blue, solid red, green with ivory band, red with ivory band, and blue with ivory band.

1939 catalog (nickel-plated tools)—green with ivory band, red with ivory band, solid green, and solid red. When no color was specified green was shipped automatically. Stainless steel tools had lacquered handles.

1941 catalog (nickel-plated tools)—solid red, solid green, red with ivory band, and green with ivory band.

1947 catalog (new chrome-plated tools, 2600 line)—plastic handles in: red, yellow, royal blue, green, and ivory.
(Nickel-plated tools, 1400 line)—green with white band, red with white band. When no color was specified, red with white band was shipped.
(Chrome-plated tools, 1600 line)—natural wooden handles.
(Nickel-plated tools, 1000 line)—solid red, solid green. When no color was specified, red was shipped.

1948 catalog (nickel-plated tools, 1000 line)—solid red, only.
(Nickel-plated tools, 1400 line)—red with white band.
(Chrome-plated tools, 1600 line)—same as 1947.
(Stainless steel tools, 3600 line)—lacquered, natural hardwood handles.
(Stainless steel tools, 1900 line)—black plastic handles.
(Stainless steel tools, 1700 line)—plastic handles offered in green, red, yellow, or blue with ivory tip and black band.

1949 catalog—the 1400 line was the last line with painted wooden handles. In 1949, the line had handles with hang-up holes. Red with white band handles were available through the 1950s. Green wooden handles were discontinued in 1947 or 1948.

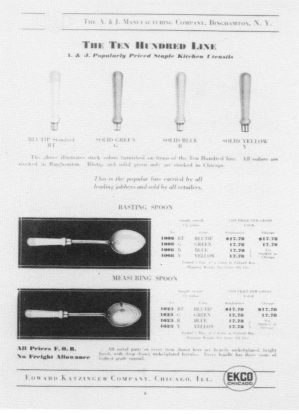

24.

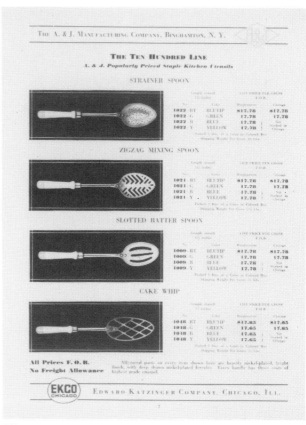

25.

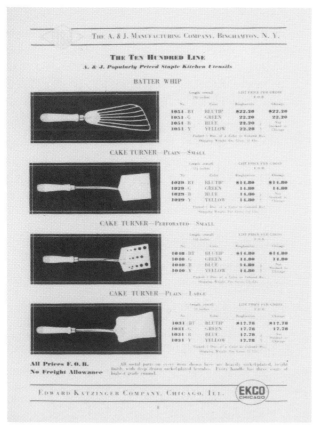

26.

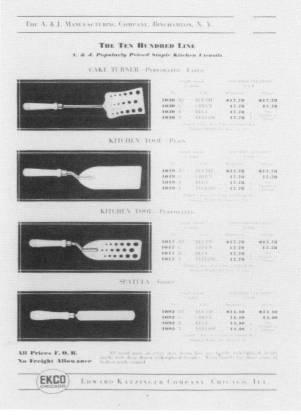

27.

28.

29.

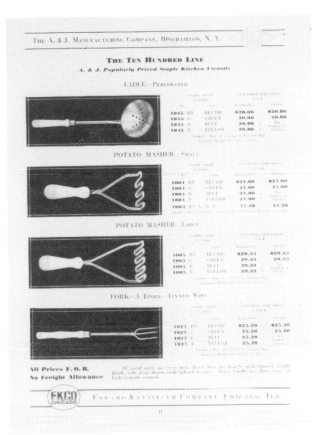

30.

31.

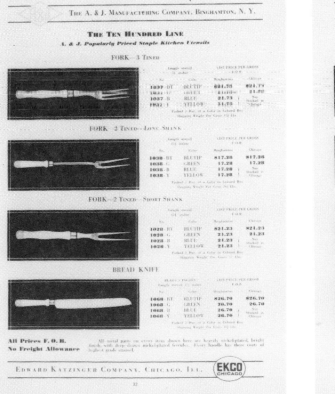

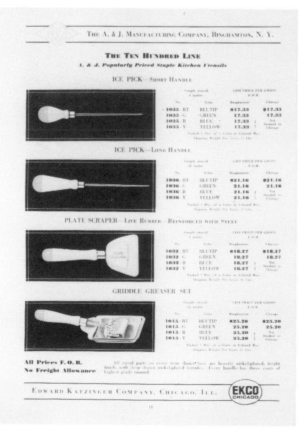

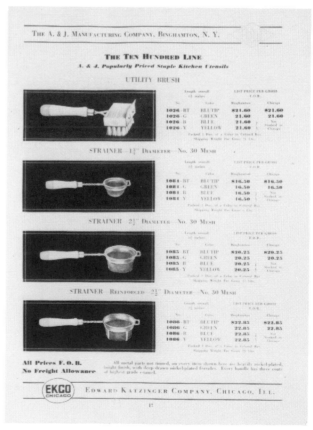

32.

33.

34.

35.

36.

37.

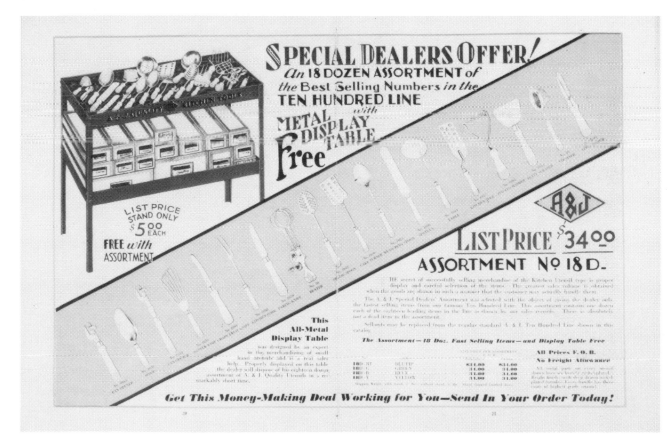

38.

39.

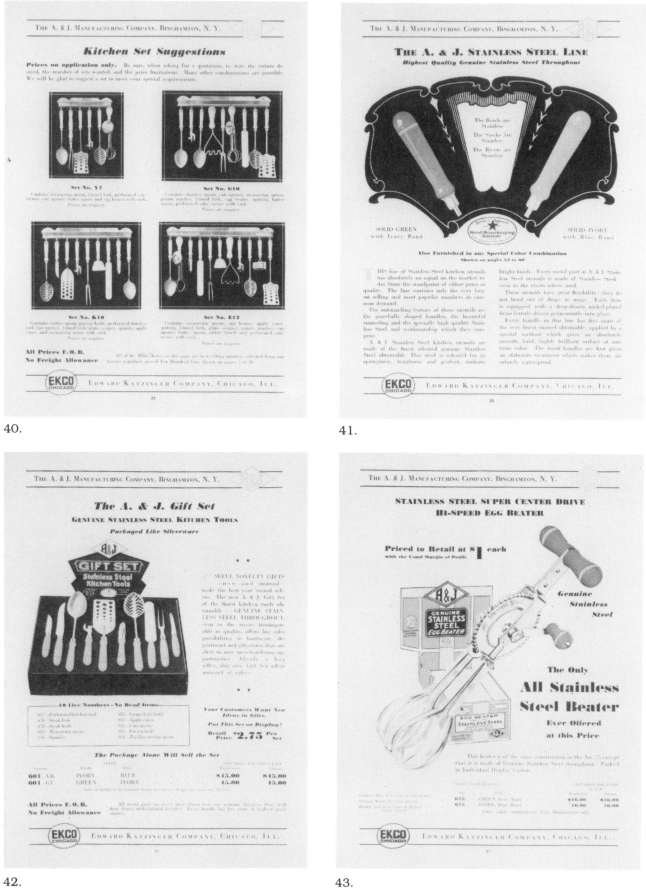

40.

41.

42.

43.

64

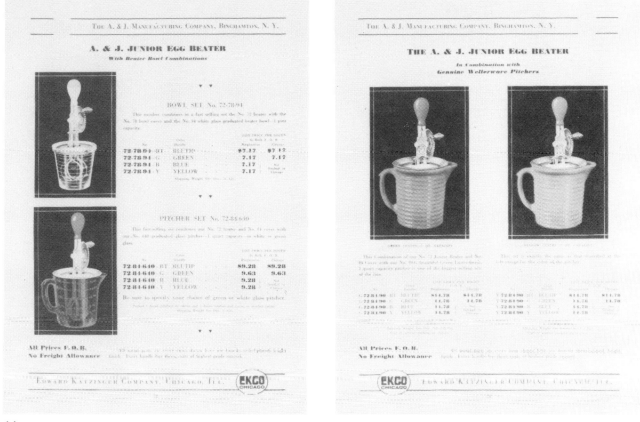

44.

45.

Androck Handles

Ferrule

1920s

Ferrule

1920s

Ferrule

Six-sided handle
Late 1920s and early 1930s

Ferrule

Used only on masher handles in the 1920s

Ferrule

"Teardrop" handle
1934 to early 1940s

A & J and ECKO

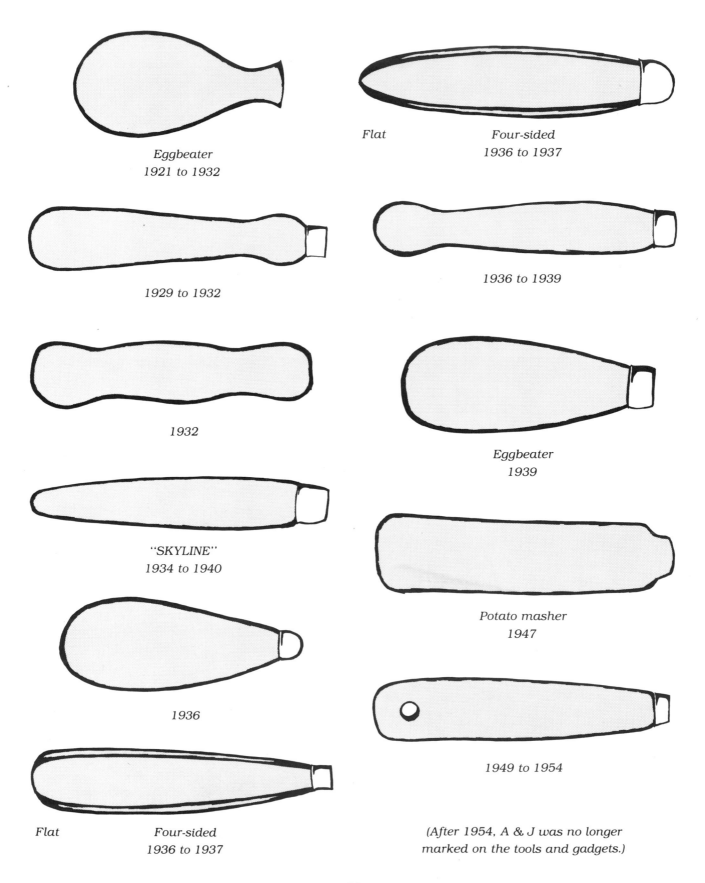

Eggbeater
1921 to 1932

Flat   Four-sided
           1936 to 1937

1929 to 1932

1936 to 1939

1932

Eggbeater
1939

"SKYLINE"
1934 to 1940

Potato masher
1947

1936

1949 to 1954

Flat   Four-sided
           1936 to 1937

(After 1954, A & J was no longer
marked on the tools and gadgets.)

Dating Patent Numbers

Patent numbers found on kitchen gadgets can be a great aid in determining the approximate age of the item in question. Under the specific authority of the Constitution, the federal government can grant exclusive rights for patents.

The first United States patent laws were adopted in 1790. When a patent is granted, the inventor has the sole right to make, use, and sell the item in question for seventeen years. It cannot be renewed except by an act of Congress.

When an invention is filed with the patent office it is permissible to have "patent pending" or "patent applied for" on the article before it is actually patented. When the patent is granted, the item will probably have either the patent number or the patent date on it. It usually took between one and two years for a patent to be granted or denied.

The intention was that once the patent was denied, the manufacturer could no longer use "patent pending" or "patent applied for." There has been some misuse of this, and it has been difficult to police, according to the U.S. patent office.

The following list shows the first patent number recorded on January 1 of each year. Many tools and gadgets from 1920 to 1950 have survived. As you will see, modern versions of many are being produced today. In addition, some tools and gadgets discontinued in past years have been reintroduced recently and have met with more success.

Date	Patent		Date	Patent
1920	1,326,899		1936	2,026,516
1921	1,364,063		1937	2,066,309
1922	1,401,948		1938	2,104,004
1923	1,440,362		1939	2,142,080
1924	1,478,996		1940	2,185,170
1925	1,521,590		1941	2,227,418
1926	1,568,040		1942	2,268,510
1927	1,612,790		1943	2,307,007
1928	1,654,521		1944	2,338,081
1929	1,696,897		1945	2,366,154
1930	1,742,181		1946	2,391,855
1931	1,787,424		1947	2,413,675
1932	1,839,190		1948	2,433,824
1933	1,892,663		1949	2,457,797
1934	1,941,449		1950	2,492,944
1935	1,985,878			to 2,536,015

Baking Tools

A 1926 cookbook stated that the temperature given for baking could be relied upon if the oven were properly preheated to the temperature stipulated in the recipe. The individual usually solved her own problems. Popular household tests were:

Sprinkling dry flour on the floor of the oven. If it browned in five minutes the temperature was between 350° and 400° and, therefore, right for plain cakes.

Placing a piece of white paper in the oven. If it browned in five minutes, a moderate oven temperature between 350° and 400° was indicated.

Holding a hand in the oven and counting. If too hot on the count of five, the oven was about 450° to 500°. If the hand could be held in to the count of eight, the oven was about 400° to 450°; to count fifteen, the temperature was right for meringues.

Cookie Cutters

Novelty cookie cutters with either colored wooden handles or colored metal handles were made during this era. In a 1921 *Good Housekeeping* magazine, Swans Down cake flour offered a set of four novelty "bridge" cookie cutters with metal handles and a copy of the new Swans Down recipe book for fifteen cents.

Metal handled cookie cutters were probably made by the Aluminum Goods Manufacturing Company (Mirro). Those in Fig. 46 were featured in *American Home* magazine in 1934. All are unmarked and have green metal handles. They were available with red handles, c. 1938.

46. These cookie cutters have metal handles. Man with hat cutter (upper left) is 6"×3½". **$1.25—4.50**

47. These cookie cutters have wooden handles. Heart shape (upper left) is 2¾"× 2⅞".
Figures: **$1.25–4.50**   Hearts: **$.50–3.00**

49. Cookie cutters with red or green painted wooden handles were made, c. 1938. Bell (center left) is 2¾"× 2¾". **$1.00–4.50**

48. Some cookie cutters with wooden handles had rivets in the center, c. 1936. Santa (left) is 2¾"× 4".
Bridge sets: **$3.00–10.00**   Other: **$1.25–4.50**

50. These 2" biscuit and doughnut cutters had green wooden handles. **$1.00–3.50**

51. Metal cake and sandwich cutters, c. 1929, were 1¾" deep with ¾" green border. Heart shape is 2¾"× 2⅞". **$3.00–5.00**

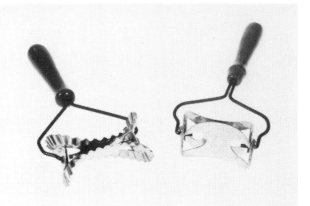

52. Revolving cookie cutters have green wooden handles. On the left is a tea wafer cutter named Roll-Em-Out™ and patented by the American Cutter Company on October 6, 1925. It measures 6½" long and has 2" × 1½" blade. The green wooden handled cutter (right) was marked: Aluminum Pat. Pending. Blades measure 2½" × 1¾"; length is 6½".
$5.00—8.50

53. Rotary cutting device has a green wooden handle. Length is 5¾"; blades measure 3" × 1⅝".
$5.00—8.50

54. Dough blenders are used to blend flour and shortening. An A & J dough blender (left) measures 4½" × 4". This was patented under patents 1,486,255, 1,645,062, 1,724,356 by C.B. Lambert in 1924, 1927, and 1929. He called it a mixer, combined food chopper, pie crust mixer, and flaker. It has five ⅛" metal blades. The Androck dough blender, c. 1927, has a green octagon wooden handle and seven wires. It measures 5½" × 4".
Marked: **$1.00—7.50**   Unmarked: **$1.50—4.00**

Revolving Cookie Cutters

When this type of cutter was pushed by its handle on a sheet of dough, the head revolved and cut a continuous pattern of cookies, using a minimum of dough. One swift motion of the rotating cutter made a whole row of wafers. The rustproof aluminum blades were easily taken apart for cleaning. They came in assorted colors. Also available were Roll-Em-Out™ molasses cookie and doughnut cutters. The cookie cutter patent, number 1,556,019 was filed on December 9, 1922, and patented October 6, 1925. Gertrude H. Newman and Frederick Hills Newman of Milwaukee, Wisconsin, were the inventors and assignors to American Cutter Company of Milwaukee, Wisconsin. Fig. 53 shows a rotary cutting device with patent number 1,885,663 which was filed January 9, 1931, and patented April 26, 1932. Invented by George J. Bregman of Cleveland, Ohio, it was described in the patent as follows: "This invention relates to rotary dough cutting devices and as its principle object aims to provide an improved and simplified device of this kind. . . ."

Dough Blenders

A dough or pastry blender has a series of parallel spring wires that are curved in a U-shape and attached to a handle. Using a pastry blender instead of the hands is thought to provide a quicker cutting in of shortening which results in a light and tender pastry dough. It can also be used to mince cooked eggs, to cream butter and sugar, and to dice berries and fruit. Green handled blenders were made in the 1920s and 1930s; red handled blenders in the 1940s.

The following are similar to Fig. 54.

An Androck blender with patent number 1,735,236 has a green wooden handle and wires. It is 5½" × 4". This was invented by Elmer L. Dennis of Rockford, Illinois. Filed on July 5, 1927, and patented November 12, 1929, the dough blender was described as follows by Dennis: "This invention relates to kitchen utensils generally but has particular reference to one designed for making pie crust where it is desired to thoroughly blend the shortening with the flour without working the same with the hands, the good blending of the dough resulting in crust of the desired flakiness. The device of my invention has been designed not only with a view to efficiency for use in the particular kind of work referred to, but also with a view to simplicity and economy in construction, durability, ease of cleaning, and adaptability, by reason of its special shape, to fit diverse shapes of mixing bowls." Another Androck blender was made with a red wooden handle, but produced c. 1941.

A Rapid Shortening™ Mixer (pat. pend.), with green wooden handle and seven wires, was similar. It measured 5¼" × 4⅛". Two other unmarked blenders with green handles have been found. Both have seven wires. One, with ribbed end, measures 5¼" × 4⅛". The other, with plain end, measures 5⅝" × 4¼". An umarked pastry brush also has a green wooden handle measuring 9¼". Brush is 3" long.

Pie Crimpers

A pie crimper, pastry crimper, dough wheel, or dough trimmer is used for trimming and marking pic crust and for sealing in juices.

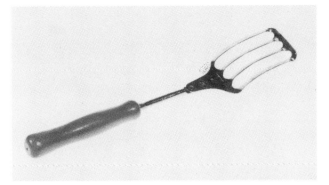

55. This A & J tool with a green wooden handle is described as a pastry blender in a 1936 A & J catalog. The blade measures 4⅛", and overall length is 10½". Marked: **$2.50—7.50**

56. Vaughan's pie trimmer and sealer (left), patent number 1,377,974, on May 10, 1921, has a wheel diameter of 2⅛" and is 6" long. The other four pie sealers have colored handles and are about the same size. Vaughan's: **$3.00—10.00** Unmarked: **$2.00—4.00**

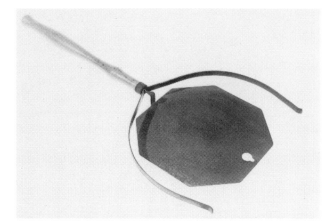

57. Pie lifter has a green wooden handle, tin lifter, and ferrule. Lifter measures 8¾" × 7½" and total length is 18". **$5.00–18.00**

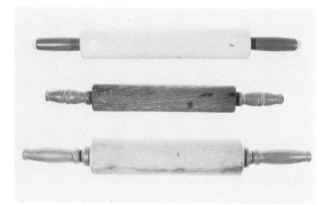

58. These rolling pins have green wooden handles. The top one (Kresge's price sticker says 15¢) measures 16" with a 9⅞" roller. The middle pin has a 10" roller and measures 16¼", while the bottom one is 19¼" with a 10" roller. **$2.00–8.50**
(Bigger pins are more expensive.)

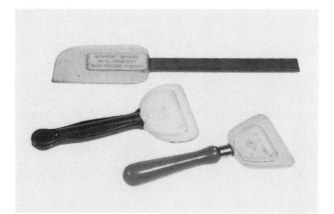

59. An A & J rubber scraper (bottom) has a green wooden handle. It has a 1⅞" × 2⅜" blade and is 6" long. The Daisy™ kitchen spatula by Schacht Rubber Manufacturing Company (top) measures 9⅛" with a 3½" × 2⅛" blade. The Daisy scraper, patent number 1,898,690 (center), has a green rubber

Rolling Pins

A rolling pin is an implement used to flatten dough in smooth, even sheets for cookies, biscuits, or pie crust. In 1930, there were various sizes priced at nineteen cents and twenty-five cents in the Sears, Roebuck Catalog. Green handled rolling pins were available before this time.

The following are similar to Fig. 58.

An unmarked pin with green wooden handles measures 15⅛" with a 9" roller.
An unmarked pin with green wooden handles measures 18" with a 10" roller.
An unmarked pin with green and natural wooden handles measures 17¼" with a 10" roller.
An unmarked pin with red and natural wooden handles measures 17¼" with a 10" roller.
An unmarked pin with red and natural wooden handles measures 17¾" with a 10¾" roller.

Rubber Spatulas and Scrapers

These are used to scrape plates, mixing bowls, pots, and pans. Similar to Fig. 59 is a scraper with U.S. patent no. 1,898,690, Aberton, Ohio. It has a green rubber handle and measures 5½" long. Blade is 1¾" × 2⅜".
An A & J plate scraper (pat. apld. for) has a white with blue tip wooden handle and measures 6". Blade is 1⅞" × 2⅜".

---

handle and measures 5¾". Blade is 2" × 2¼". Clifford A. Schacht filed this on August 27, 1932, and patented it on February 21, 1933, as a dish scraper. He said, *This invention is a novel improvement in dish or sink scrapers and the like such as shown in my U.S. letters patent number 1,747,751 dated November 1, 1927, and the principle object there is to provide a scraper molded in one piece having a flexible blade and an integral reinforced hard or inflexible blade and an integral reinforced hard or inflexible rubber handle extending partially into the blade, the scraper, or the like. Heretofore, scrapers have been used having flexible rubber blades, but the handles theretofore have been made of metal, wood, or the like, attached to the blade by different methods and means, but such scrapers have been found unsatisfactory and unsanitary in that the handles eventually become loose and cut or tear the rubber blade and moreover it is impossible to keep the connection between the handle and the scraper free from dirt, grease, food and other germ carrying mediums....* **$2.00–4.00**

Beaters and Whippers

There are fixed, mechanical, and rotary beaters and whippers. Fixed tools operate solely by the motion of the arm. Similar to Fig. 60 is a 7¾" spiral whisk with 1¼" green wooden knob. A flat whip is used to beat egg whites on a platter, to mix cream or egg yolk in a shallow pan, or to attack lumps along the edge of the pan.

Mechanical beaters, which operate like a spinning top, have an up-and-down motion. Hold it by the knob on top, push down, and the spiral shaft turns the wired whisk at the bottom; lift the knob, and the whisk turns in the opposite direction. The beater functions easily and will beat eggs, whip cream, or make milk shakes.

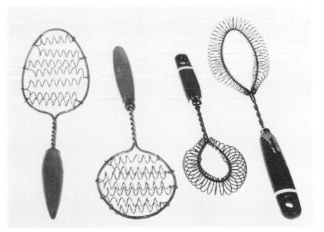

60. The 8" spiral whisk (left) has a green wooden handle which is 5⅞". The 9⅝" whisk (right) marked Siegler on one side and Warm Floor Heaters on the other has a 4⅝" red wooden handle. **$1.50–3.50**

61. The flat wire whip, probably by Androck (left), has a 4¼" green teardrop handle and measures 10⅞". The unmarked flat wire whip (center left) has a six-sided, green wooden handle measuring 4⅝". Total length is 12". The unmarked oval, coiled flat whip (center right) has a red wooden handle with ivory band and hang-up hole (A & J). Total length is 9¼". Handle is 3⅞". The unmarked oval, coiled flat whip (right) has a red wooden handle with ivory band and hang-up hole (A & J). It measures 11¾" with a 4¼" handle. **$1.50–3.50**

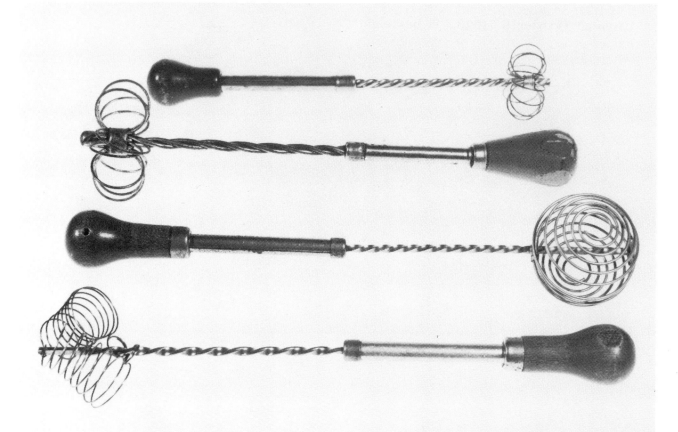

62. The green handled whisk (top) was marked Steelcraft Germany British Zone and measures 9½". A whisk (bottom) made in England under patent 8136 has a red wooden knob and measures 10¾". Another whisk (second from top) was made in England under the same patent and has a green wooden knob. An unmarked whisk with a green wooden handle (third from top) measures 11¾".

$2.00—5.00

63. One-hand, automatic eggbeater by EKCO first appeared in the 1959 EKCO catalog for sixty-nine cents. It has four-winged beater, red wooden handle with ivory band and hang-up hole. Length is 10⅝".
$1.50—3.50

Similar to Fig. 62 is an unmarked whisk with red wooden handle. It is 11⅜" long.

Similar to Fig. 63 is another beater with four wings and lemon yellow with black band and ivory tipped wooden handle with hang up hole. Length is 10⅝".

Rotary beaters operate by geared wheels which rotate the blade(s). They are used to beat or whip eggs, sauces, and other semi-liquid mixtures. There are two types—winged beaters and turbine cream and egg whips.

The A & J winged beater was invented by Charles E. Kail, Binghamton, New York, assignor to A & J Manufacturing Company, Binghamton, New York. The application was filed on May 2, 1922, and patent was granted October 9, 1923, under numbers 1,470,169 and 1,470,170.

Similar to Fig. 64 is an A & J beater patented October 9, 1923. It has eight wings, vertical green wooden handle and crank, and perforated gear wheel. Length is 11⅝".

Another A & J beater patented October 9, 1923, has four wings, vertical green wooden handle, metal crank, and perforated gear wheel. Length is 10⅞". A third A & J beater patented October 9, 1923, has four wings, vertical green wooden handle, metal crank, and solid gear wheel. Length is 10¾".

Another A & J beater patented October 9, 1923, has four wings, vertical green wooden handle, metal crank, and perforated gear wheel. Length is 10⅞".

A similar A & J beater patented October 9, 1923, has four wings, vertical blue wood handle, metal crank, and solid gear wheel. Length is 10⅞".

Similar to Fig. 65 is a A & J beater with four wings, red wooden handle, metal crank, and solid gear wheel. Length is 5¾".

Fig. 66 is a high speed, super center drive, A & J beater with solid gear wheel and bronze bearings, c. 1934. It has eight wings, green wooden "T" handle and crank. Length is 11½". This high speed, center drive beater carries patent 2,049,727. Application was filed on June 13, 1934, and patent granted August 4, 1936. The inventor was Myron J. Zimmer, Chicago, Illinois, assignor to Edward Katzinger Company, Chicago, Illinois. Zimmer said, "This invention relates to new and useful improvements in gear hubs and has for its object a construction wherein the hub is an integral and unitary part of the gear body and may be inexpensively created and formed. . . ." The company made a stainless steel, super center drive, HI-SPEED eggbeater in 1930 that retailed for one dollar. The 1935 patent apparently is an improvement on this beater.

Another high speed beater made by A & J is of stainless steel. It has eight wings, green wooden D-shaped handle and crank, c. 1934. Length is 12".

A high-speed A & J beater made by Ekco Products Co. has eight wings, natural and black wooden D-shaped handle with ivory band and natural wooden crank. Length is 12½". This was manufactured after World War II.

64. This 11¾" A & J rotary beater, c. 1922, has a vertical, white wooden handle and crank; solid gear wheel, and eight wings. **$2.50–14.00**

65. About 1941, A & J made a green wooden handled beater (left) which was marked on gear wheel, "BEATS ANYTHING in a Cup or Bowl." Made for only one or two years, this four-winged beater was listed in the Edward Katzinger and A & J kitchen tools 1941 catalog. The A & J beater patented October 8, 1923, has four wings, green wooden handle, metal crank, and solid gear wheel. It is 5¾" long. This small portion eggbeater was mounted on a card. It was nickel plated and had a solid green handle. This quote is from A & J Kitchen Tool Co.-Edward Katzinger Co., 1935. The last listing for this beater was in 1939 catalog. *This Midget egg beater is designed to fill the need for a beater to whip small portions of cream, beat a single egg or mix a small portion of mayonnaise. 1 wing midget beater $.72. Weight per dozen 1½" lbs. Packed 1 dozen to Box.* **$2.50–14.00**

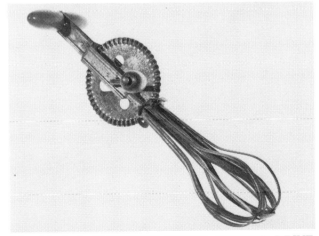

66. Marked, "HI-SPEED SUPER CENTER DRIVE PAT APL'D FOR A & J," c. 1934, beater has eight wings and a green wooden, pointed "T" handle and crank. Length is 11¾". **$2.50–6.00**

67. Androck made this beater with green wooden handle and three white bands, c. 1929. It features eight wings, natural wooden crank, and solid gear wheel. Length is 12¼″. **$2.50–8.00**

68. Edlund made D-shaped wooden handle beaters, c. 1929. Beater on left has eight wings, green handle and crank. Length is 11¾″. Beater on right is stainless steel with red D-shaped wooden handle and crank. Length is 12¾″. The display cover says, *Edlund Extra Strong Bearings and Stainless Steel Blades Gears Mesh thru wheel — Can't Slip!* (on one side) *Edlund Easily Rinsed Clean. No dents for food to hide. Brass bearing for longer life. Heavy duty. Model No. 0.* **$2.00–6.00**

Similar to Fig. 67 is an Androck beater, patent number 1,767,454. It has solid gear wheel, eight wings, vertical, green wooden handle and crank, and length of 12½″. The inventor was Samuel T. Hobbs of Worcester, Massachusetts, assignor to the Washburn Company of Worcester, Massachusetts. This variation was filed on August 9, 1929, and patented on June 24, 1930.

Beater similar to Fig. 68 is from Edlund Company, patent number 1,789,224. This stainless steel beater has eight wings, green D-shaped wooden handle and crank, and length of 12″. Under the same patent number was an Edlund beater with eight wings, vertical green wooden handle and crank, and length of 11⅝″. Patent number 1,789,224 was filed on November 18, 1929, by the inventor Henry J. Edlund and patented on January 13, 1931. The object of this invention was to provide an improved form of drive wheel and gear construction, to provide beater blades that could be easily cleaned and maintained in a sanitary condition, and to provide a handle which was easy to grip and which would permit the beater to be held rigidly without great effort on the part of the operator.

69. Ladd beater with eight wings, green wooden crank, and D-shaped handle was patented by United Royalties Corporation, October 18, 1921. Length is 11½". **$1.50–4.50**

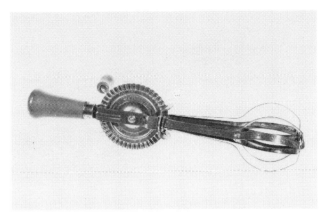

70. The Taplin Manufacturing Company made a beater with eight wings and vertical, green wooden handle and crank, patented December 9, 1924. Length is 11⅛". **$2.50–8.00**

United Royalties promoted Ladd beaters like this: "Throw Away Your Old Balky Beater: Then try one of the beautifully nickeled LADD Beaters with a whirlwind wheel, that runs as smoothly as a clock—on genuine ball bearings. The LADD is the only Ball Bearing Beater made. The 8 blades whirl so fast they blur on the vision. This unusual speed improves the flavor of icings, dressings, beverages, light batters, etc., by mixing ingredients more thoroughly. And what is equally important—faster beating aerates the mixture, giving it that fluffy lightness which makes foods additionally tempting, healthful, and delicious." Both white and colored handles were available.

Similar to Fig. 69 is a beater marked, "LADD PAT'S Nov. 30-26, Nov. 1-27, Jul. 3-28, Apr. 16-29 STAINLESS," with eight wings, horizontal, green wooden handle and crank, and length of 11¼".

Another Ladd beater patented October 18, 1921, has eight wings, vertical, white wooden handle, metal crank, and length of 11".

The Taplin beater was invented by George Wessell of Brooklyn, New York. Application was filed on August 18, 1921, and patent was granted December 9, 1924. Similar to Fig. 70 is another Taplin beater with eight wings, vertical, green wooden handle and crank, and length of 11½". It was patented December 9, 1924. The Taplin beater with patent number 1,518,285 has four wings, vertical, red wooden handle and crank, and length of 11".

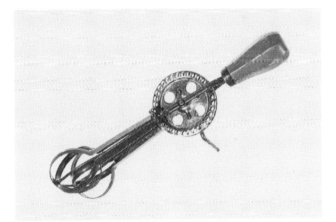

71. Whip-Well™ beater has eight wings, green wooden handle and metal crank. Length is 11". It was patented March 23, 1920 and May 21, 1921. **$2.50–8.00**

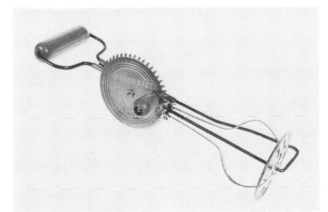

72. A & J Superspeed Spinnit™ cream and egg whip first appeared in the 1940 catalog, reappeared in the 1947 catalog, but was not in the 1948 catalog. It is 11½" long and has a green wooden handle and crank. **$2.00–7.00**

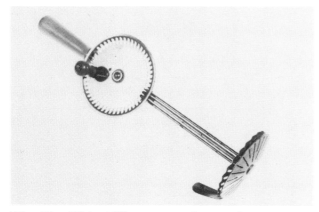

73. The Whippit™ cream and egg whip is 13¼"
long and has a green wooden handle and crank. Duro
Metal Products Company sold it for one dollar in
1927. The Whippit trademark was registered by
White and Hallock, Inc., Muskegon, Michigan, on
September 18, 1928. It had been used by their pre-
decessor since July 15, 1925. In 1945, EKCO
acquired the patent, and listed it in the 1947 catalog
as the Whippit cream whip. *Cream colored Enameled Handles. Super-speed cream whip, it beats,
mixes in any size or shape bowl. Patented guard
prevents splash. Double action, turbine type blade,
shaped to fit any size bowl. Nickel plated. In three
color box — individually packed,* read the catalog
description. **$6.50–15.00**

74. Cream and egg whipper by Duplex-Whipper
Corporation measures 12½" and has a green wooden
handle and crank. It was patented in 1919.
$2.50–8.00

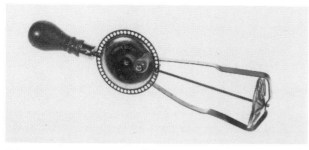

75. The 11" Turbine™ beater patented by the
Washburn Company features a green vertical handle
and crank. **$2.00–12.50**

76. This beater with a vertical, green wooden
handle and crank measures 9¾". **$2.50–8.00**

Similar to Fig. 75 is the BEATS ALL™ by
The Washburn Co. It measures 11" and
has a green wooden handle and crank. The
Androck Turbine Beater is 11¼" and has a
vertical, green wooden handle and crank.

Beater and Bowl or Pitcher Sets

A & J Manufacturing Company made beater
and bowl or pitcher sets from 1924 to 1959.
The pitchers and bowls were offered in clear
and colored glass or stoneware. In the beginning these were made by Federal Glass Company and Universal Pottery. After a few years,
Hazel-Atlas Glass Company and Weller Pottery
began to manufacture these items for A & J and
continued to do so until 1959, when only two
kinds were available. A & J patented a number
of beater sets under the same date—October 9,
1923.

77. Patented October 9, 1923 by A & J, this beater and pitcher set has eight wings, metal lid, green wooden handle and crank, and measures 11½". The one-quart pitcher, graduated in ounces, cups, and pints, is green glass. The unit measures 12".
$9.00—16.00

78. This EKCO A & J clear glass pitcher is graduated in ounces and cups, measuring two cups total. The beater has four wings and a red wooden handle with metal crank and lid. Pitcher is trademarked with ECKO and A & J No. 7218 on bottom. Overall height is 10". **$9.00—16.00**

Fig. 77 is a one-quart version. Another, a one-pint size, had a four-wing beater, green wooden handle with ivory tip and band, and clear glass bowl with two-ounce gradations. Overall height was 11¼".

Merry Whirl™, patented November 28, 1916, is similar to Fig. 78 which is an ECKO A & J product. The one-quart clear glass pitcher has gradations in ounces and cups and is marked T & S Torrington on the bottom. Beater has eight wings, red wooden handle and crank, metal lid, and the set is 12" high.

A & J produced two other beater sets also bearing the October 9, 1923, trademark date, which are not pictured. The one-pint size has four wings, a green wooden handle, metal crank and lid, and measures 11" high. The other, a one-quart version with eight-winged beater, features a D-shaped, red wooden handle and crank, metal lid, and is 11¾" high.

79. H over A is the trademark appearing on the bottom of this bowl, which is graduated in ounces and cups to a two-cup capacity. The four-wing beater, labeled T & S No. 39 has a vertical, green wooden handle and metal crank and lid. Overall height is 12". **$9.00—16.00**

80. Beater set labeled with the Full/Vision logo on the gear wheel and the clamp, and A & J under the clamp. It has four wings, red wooden handle, metal crank, and measures 9½″ overall. This design was a combination of the A & J rotary beater with four wings and the A & J rotary sifter. It proved unpopular and was discontinued, which makes it a valuable collectible. The 1941 A & J EKCO catalog said: *A & J all metal beater set. Full/Vision egg beater set. Red enameled handle only. No cover — no spatter — no splash. 1½″ pint unbreakable, all metal bowl beater unit can be used separately. Four tinned wings — wire supports — side drive — spiral wire gear knob. Ingredients can be added while beating operation is in progress. All metal bowl can be used several ways in kitchen. A practical, compact beating unit that is not a toy.* **$9.00—16.00**

81. Two Androck turbine beaters feature metal lids and red wooden cranks. The unit on left has opaque glass and stands 7″ tall, c. 1940. The one on the right has clear glass, one-half cup bowl and is 6″ high. **$9.00—16.00**

The Androck bowls in Fig. 81 were marked ANDROCK MADE IN U.S.A. The beater on the left was marked ANOTHER ANDROCK PRODUCT Pat. No. 2,210,810 and the one on right ANDROCK PATENT PENDING. This is earlier model.

Chicago Precision Products Corporation also manufactured another turbine beater with red wooden crank, metal lid, clear glass bowl, and an overall height of 4½". It is quite similar to Fig. 82.

82. Chicago Precision Products Corporation made this turbine beater with clear glass bowl, red wooden crank and metal lid. Overall height is 6".

$9.00—16.00

83. This beater was invented by Irving Machumson and patented November 21, 1933, by Vidrio Products Corporation. The electric unit has a motor that slows down considerably as the cream being whipped thickens. It has a green glass, one pint graduated measuring container, patent number 1,935,857. The motor's 4½" handle is green wood, and there is a single, two-winged beater. Overall height is 7". The motor operates on 110-125 volt, AC only.

$3.50—16.50

81

Bottle, Can, and Jar Openers, Lifters and Wrenches

Bottle cap removers will remove anchor and friction tops, open press-in tops, loosen glass jar covers, and remove all bottle caps.

Similar to Fig. 84 is a Pickwick Ale opener by Edlund Co. It has a green wooden handle and is 4⅝" long.

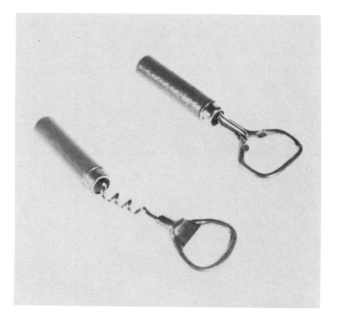

85.   The George Worthington 1936 catalog said this about the unmarked bottle opener and corkscrew with green wooden handle (left): *PAL combination cork screw and cap lifter, nickel plated, inserted in a ferruled green or red tube. Malleable opener, steel cork screw.* The unmarked bottle opener and cork-screw (right) has a red wooden handle. It measures 3⅝" with a 1⅛" screw.   **$2.00–5.00**

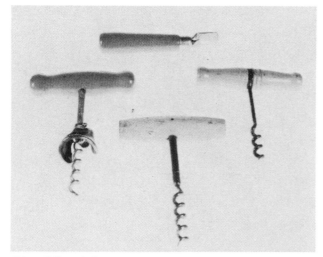

84.   Edlund Company patented this bottle opener (top) on November 7, 1933. It has a green wooden handle and measures 4½".   **$1.00–4.50**
These unmarked corkscrew openers have green wooden handles also. The one with metal guard (left) is 4¾" long, c. 1936. The one on the right, c. 1937, has the corkscrew attached around the handle.
$2.00–6.00

A corkscrew, a tool with spiral threads attached to a handle, is used for removing corks from bottles. The spiral pierces the cork, and the operator twists it to remove the cork.

86. MS Company appeared on the shaft of this bottle and jar opener (left). It measures 5⅞″ long. The bottle, can, and jar opener (right) measures 8⅛″ long. Both have green wooden handles. **32.00–6.00**

Manual Can Openers

With manual, crank-operated can openers, a push of the lever places the knife and a few turns of the crank cuts off the can lid completely with no ragged edges.

Similar to Fig. 88 is a Miracle™ can opener with a green, four-sided wooden handle and 6⅝″ length.

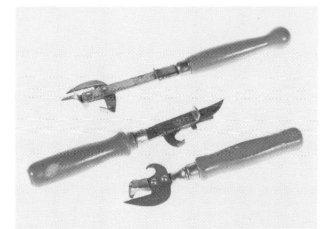

87. The puncturing point and cutting blade is used to open cans with these manual can openers with vacuum cap removers. An A & J steel tempered opener (top) with green wooden handle measures 8⅛″. A & J made a similar tool with a smaller ferrule and another that was only 6½″. The bottom opener, marked stainless, is 6″. Acme made an opener with a red wooden handle which was 6⅞″. Safe-T-Manufacturing Company made one 5⅞″ opener with a green handle. **$1.00–2.50**

88. Two green handled A & J MIRACLE™ can openers measure 6¼″ (left) and 4¼″ (center). The Miracle trademark has been used since November 18, 1932. The Miracle can opener has been the number one product of EKCO since the 1930s. The Taplin Manufacturing Company made this 6⅛″ can opener (right) with green wooden handle, patent number 2,058,875, in 1937. **$1.00–3.00**

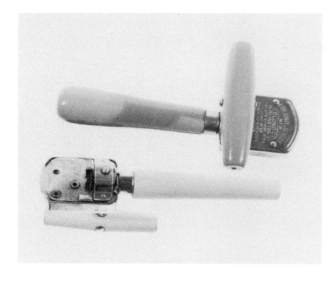

89. This Edlund Junior #5™ can opener was patented April 21-May 12, 1925, and June 18, 1929. The user must keep clean and oil regularly, said directions on the bottom. This tool has a green wooden handle, 3¼″ green crank and is 6¼″ long. A later version (bottom) has a yellow handle. A 1929 *Good Housekeeping* ad said: *Easy As Cutting Butter — A joy in the kitchen. Opening cans — bane of kitchen chores — surrenders readily to this smooth-working, new type can opener. Round, square, oval cans, large or small, are opened without a struggle by the Edlund Jr., leaving a smooth, safe edge. The same mechanical principles that made Edlund can openers the standard in restaurants and hotels the world over are now brought to the household kitchen in this attractive, compact, lifetime utensil. Treat yourself to an Edlund Jr., Can Opener-75¢, at all quality stores. . . . There's a new Edlund egg beater, too-75¢. If your dealer is not supplied, we will mail either or both, postpaid, with our guarantee of satisfaction.* **$2.50–3.50**

Similar to Fig. 90 is a Zim Deluxe can opener by Zim Manufacturing Co. It has a red wooden knob and is 6½″ long.

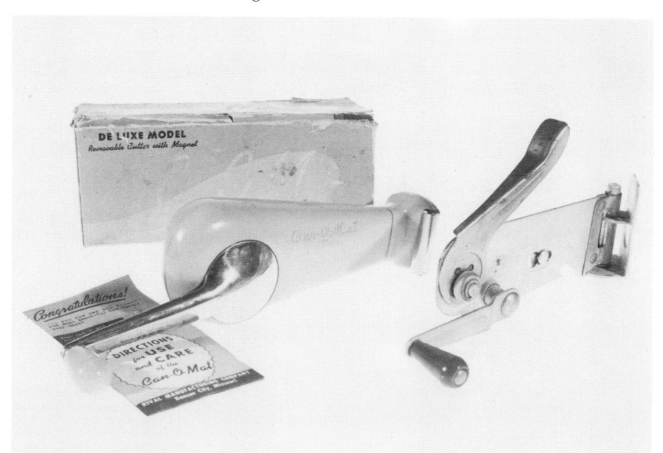

90. The Can-O-Mat™ (left) by Rival Manufacturing Company is a 7½″ wall can opener of apple green metal with a plastic crank knob. (Patent numbers D139,873; 2,378,090; 238,929.) This opener, c. 1946, was the first hand-crank, "positive single action" can opener to have its mechanism enclosed in a casing. A 6½″ can opener with red crank knob (right) made by Swing-A-Way Manufacturing Company was the first retractible wall-bracket mounted can opener. It swung left or right and was introduced in 1940. **$3.50–6.50**

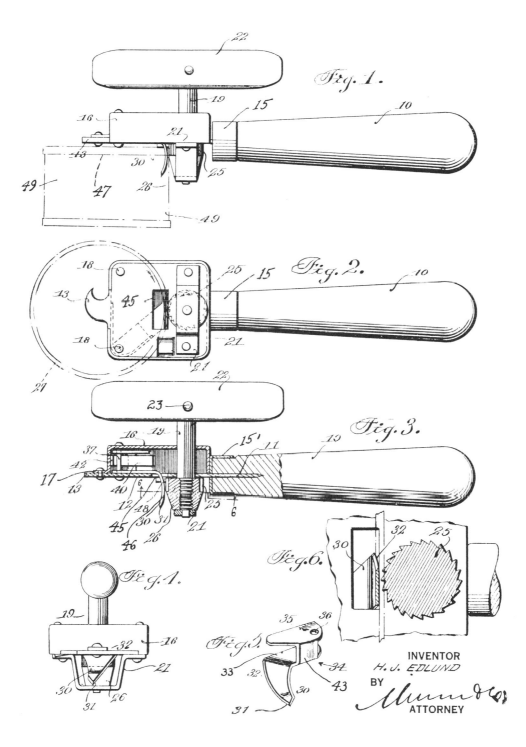

91. This schematic drawing is of an Edlund can opener.

85

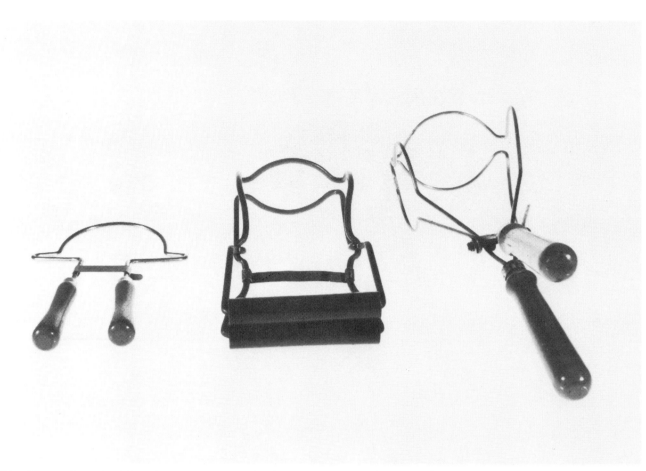

92. These three jar lifters have green wooden handles. Patented lifter (left) is 7⅜″ × 4¾″. Lifter, by Yo-Ho (center) of Monticello, Iowa, is 8″ × 3¾″. An unmarked jar lifter and holder for pints and quarts (right) is 12½″ × 3¾″. **$4.00–6.50**

Jar Lifters

A jar lifter is a device to lift a jar from boiling water or to hold a jar while fastening the lid.

Similar to center lifter in Fig. 92 is a PRESTO™ lifter with green wooden handles. It measures 7¾″ × 3⅞″.

Jar Openers and Wrenches

A jar opener or wrench is used for tightening or loosening a metal screw type top.

Similar to Fig. 94 are two unmarked rubber covered wrenches with green wooden handles. One measures 7⅛″ × 3¾″. One is 8″ × 4¾″. *Better Homes & Gardens* magazine, November, 1929, said, "The use of rubber rings with 'ears' is a help but even so the patented openers are usually worthy time-savers. . . ."

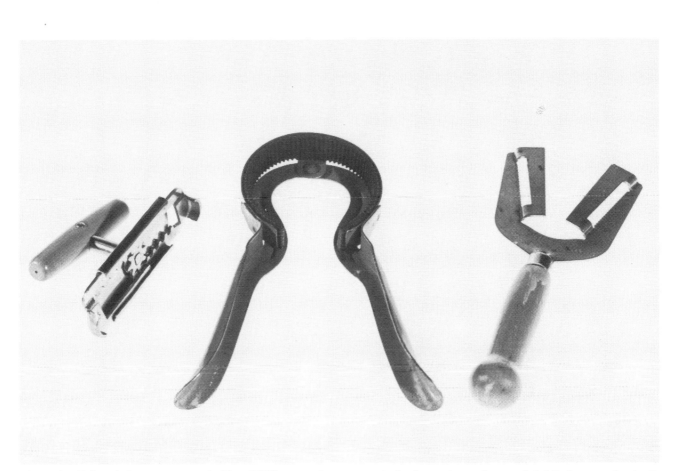

93. The Edlund Company made Top-Off™ jar and bottle screw top openers (left), patent number 1,894,556, with an apple green wooden handle (shown), red handle, and light green handle.

It was invented by H. J. Edlund. The filing date was March 18, 1932, with the patent date on January 17, 1933. Edlund said, *This invention relates to a device for removing screw threaded tops from jars or bottles. An object of the invention is the provision of a device having movable jaws which will automatically adjust themselves to screw tops of various diameters whether the tops had been applied to jars or bottles and will automatically grip the top by rotation of a handle and cause the same to be released. . . .*

Good Housekeeping magazine, April, 1933,

reported, *An extremely useful kitchen gadget. It can be fitted over screw-tops of almost every size, and a slight turn of the handle is all that is necessary to loosen the most stubborn cover from the jar or bottle, thus it saves time, and spares your disposition.* **$2.00–5.00**

The 8″ metal jar wrench and threader (center) has green enameled steel handles and corrugated rubber lining. Roger Sannipoli, of Detroit, Michigan, was the inventor. Application was filed on January 6, 1934, and patent granted on April 23, 1935. It was built to require only a light pressure on the handles for tightening or loosening jar covers. The Grip-All™ screw cap opener (right) opens and closes all sizes. It is 8″ long and blade is 3¾″. **$1.00–6.50**

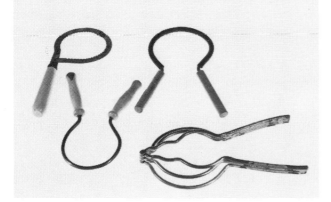

94. The rubber covered wrench (top right) measures 7¼″ and has green wooden handles. Another type of opener had three different metal wrenches hinged at the top and green metal handles soldered together (bottom right). An adjustable metal wrench (top left), c. 1936, measures 8⅜″ and has green wooden handles. An unmarked metal wrench with green wooden handles (bottom left) is 8″.

$2.00–6.50

87

Choppers and Mincers

There are hand, mechanical, and rotary hand choppers and mincers. They are used for chopping meats, eggs, herbs and fruits and vegetables.

Similar to Fig. 96 is an unmarked chopper with horizontal, green wooden handle and double curved blades. It measures $4\frac{5}{8}'' \times 5\frac{3}{8}''$.

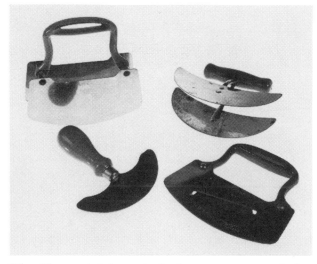

95. These stainless steel choppers are made by Acme M.G.M. Company. Top left chopper has double blades, green metal handle and is $5\frac{1}{4}'' \times 5\frac{1}{2}''$.
$5.00–9.50

Top right chopper has double curved blades and horizontal, green wooden handles. It is $4\frac{7}{8}'' \times 5\frac{1}{2}''$.
$2.25–5.00

Bottom left chopper has curved single blade and vertical, green wooden handle. It is $5\frac{1}{4}'' \times 4\frac{3}{8}''$.
$2.00–5.00

Bottom right chopper has single blade, red metal handle and is $5\frac{1}{4}'' \times 5\frac{1}{2}''$. **$3.00–7.00**

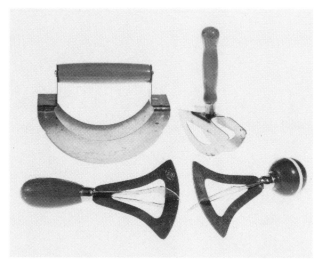

96. Pictured are A & J choppers. Top left chopper has horizontal, green wooden handle and double curved blades, c. 1936. It is $4\frac{1}{2}'' \times 5\frac{1}{2}''$.

Top right chopper has vertical, green wooden handle and double curved blades, c. 1936. It is $5\frac{5}{8}'' \times 4''$.

Bottom left mincer has vertical, red wooden handle and four-blade mincer and chopper. It is $6\frac{1}{4}'' \times 3''$.

Bottom right mincer has red with ivory band wooden knob and four-blade mincer and chopper. It is $5\frac{1}{2}'' \times 3\frac{1}{2}''$. **$2.00–9.50**

Another unmarked chopper with a horizontal, green handle with metal band in the middle and a single blade is 3⅜″ × 4½″.

An unmarked chopper with vertical, green wooden handle and single blade measures 4″ × 3¾″.

An unmarked four-blade mincer and chopper with vertical, green wooden handle measures 6″ × 3″.

Similar to Fig. 97 is an unmarked chopper with two intersecting curved blades and vertical, green wooden handle. It is 4¾″ × 4″.

The November, 1929, issue of *Better Homes & Gardens* describes the hand chopper and container as "A tearless onion chopper, consisting of a glass tumbler, a wooden disc which fits neatly into the bottom of the tumbler, and a metal cover equipped with a four-bladed knife. The name of the chopper describes only one of its many spheres of usefulness. It serves admirably for mincing small quantities of pimientoes, mushrooms, nutmeats, or hard-cooked eggs. The chief advantage is that neither the food nor the odor can escape, as in an open chopping bowl."

Similar to Fig. 98 is an Androck stainless steel chopper with 3⅜″ metal lid; 1⅞″ horizontal, red wooden handle and four-blade knife. Clear glass jar is marked H over A and is 4″ × 3⅛″. Overall height is 6⅝″; two wooden discs are marked "for onions only" and "for other foods." They are 2⅜″ in diameter.

97. An unmarked chopper and mincer has two intersecting curved blades and round, green wooden handle. The wooden bowl is 5½″ × 5½″. Unit is 4¼″ × 3⅞″. **$2.50–5.50**

98. An unmarked chopper has a horizontal, green wooden 1⅞″ handle; green metal 3⅛″ lid, and four-bladed knife. The clear glass jar is marked H over A and is 4″ × 3⅛″. Overall height is 6⅝″. Two wooden discs are marked "for onions only" and "for other foods." **$3.25–10.00**

99. Chicago Precision Products Corporation made this ice chopper with vertical, green wooden handle; metal blades, and green metal lid. It is 10"×3⅜". Clear glass jar with green enameled design is 7⅞"×3⅛". Overall height is 10¾".

$3.25—10.00

100. Foley made this chopper with stainless steel blades, patent number 2,113,085. It has a red wooden handle and is 7⅞"×3¾". **$2.50—15.00**

A mechanical spring action chopper is operated by pushing down on the handle. Foley manufactured several spring-operated choppers. One, similar to Fig. 100, is marked MPLS 8 PAT 2,113,085 on both sides, has a green wooden handle, and measures 7⅞" × 3¾". The inclusion of the postal zone in the marking would indicate that this model was produced after the chopper pictured. Foley produced another chopper, identically marked with MPLS 8 PAT 2,113,085, and the same in every respect except it possesses a differently shaped green wooden handle.

This chopper was invented by M. Higgs. Application was filed on December 21, 1935, and patent was granted on April 5, 1938. Higgs called it, "a food chopper so made that it will cut vegetables or fruits in strips, squares, or in fine pieces, and can be used in a chopping bowl or on a flat board. . . ."

Similar to Fig. 101 is an unmarked, spring action chopper with red wooden knob, red metal lid, clear glass graduated 1½-cup jar, and H over A trademark. It is 10½" × 3⅛".

Rotary Choppers

A rotary chopper is used by turning a crank. It chops nuts, raisins, or other foods.

Similar to Fig. 102 is an Androck nut meat chopper, patent number 2,001,075. It has ivory metal hopper, red wooden knob on handle, clear glass base and H over A trademark. It measures 6½" × 2¼". Another Androck nut meat chopper with patent number 2,001,075 has red metal hopper, red wooden knob on handle, clear glass base and H over A trademark. It measures 6½" × 2¼".

This nut chopper was invented by Carl A. Sundstrand, Rockford, Illinois. It was filed on November 21, 1932, and patented on May 14, 1935. He described it as "a new improved device for chopping or breaking up nut meats or other food stuffs. Despite all the ingenuity that has been exercised in the development of numerous articles of kitchenware, it appears nothing practical has been developed for breaking nut meats, as a result, this and other work of that nature has been done to a large extent by hand. The customary practice is

(continued)

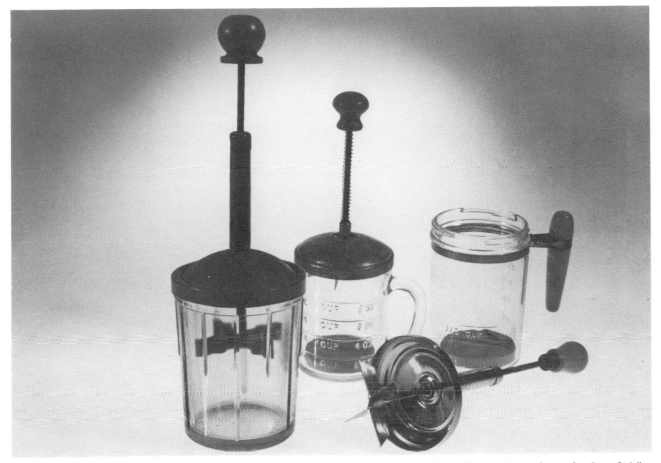

101. Lorraine Metal Manufacturing Company, Inc., made this green metal push chopper (left) with green wooden knob and green glass jar. It is 12¼″ × 3⅝″, and it sold for sixty-five cents in the 1930 Sears Roebuck catalog. **$3.50–7.50**

An unmarked spring action chopper (center) has a green wooden knob and a clear glass, graduated one-cup pitcher with an H over A trademark. It is 9¼″ × 3⅛″. **$3.25–10.00**

A stainless steel onion and nut chopper with a vertical, pink wooden knob; 3⅛″ metal lid; 1½″ handle, and four-blade knife is marked H over A. The clear glass jar has a vertical grip, pink handle, and is 4″ × 3⅛″. Overall height is 12¾″. **$3.25–10.00**

102. A rotary chopper, patent number 2,001,075 (left), has a green metal chopper with decal on front, green wooden knob for handle, and a clear glass base marked H over A. It is 6½″ × 2¼″. **$3.25–10.00**

An unmarked chopper (right center) has a red metal top, metal crank, and a clear glass base. It is 6″ × 3½″. The label on the jar reads, *Nut meat container—chopper—dispenser. Put nut meats into glass jar. To use, remove cap, invert jar and turn handle. Nut meats are chopped and dispensed in same operation; can be sprinkled into dish or into food. Unused nut meats can be kept in jar.* Federal. **$2.00–8.50**

An unmarked chopper (left center) has a red metal lid, red wooden knob on crank and clear glass base. It is 6⅛″ × 2⅛″. **$2.00–8.50**

Chopper marked Federal Tool Corporation, Chicago A 4, has a red plastic top graduated from 1 teaspoon to two tablespoons and a metal crank. It is 7½″ × 2⅛″. **$2.00–8.50**

91

103. This food chopper is a Deluxe #10 by New Standard Corporation. It has a green wooden handle, green metal crank, and it measures 8¾"×2". The attached illustration card says, *Four-way knife assembly: #1—Position cuts coarse. Use for chicken, meats, lobsters, for salads; bread and onions for stuffing; vegetables and fruits of all kinds not required in small pieces.*
#2—Position cuts medium. Used for hash, fish cakes, corn for fritters, fruits for mince meats and raw or cooked meats. Number 2 position is recommended for most all purposes.
#3—Position cuts fine. Used principally for crumbing crackers and dry bread and for grating coconuts, horseradish, and other meats and vegetables wanted very fine.
#4—Position cuts very fine. Not intended to cut hard dry goods. Used mostly for making peanut butter or similar foods required extremely fine.
$2.00—8.50

104. Rotary mincer (left) has a green wooden handle and measures 7¼"×3". Rotary mincer (right) has a green wooden handle with ferrule and measures 7¾"×3". **$2.25—7.00**

to have the nuts in a chopping bowl and to keep working them with a knife or chopper until they are brought to the desired fineness. This, as stated before, is tedious, and there is the objection that the stuff is not cut to uniform size—some particles being cut very fine and others being left very coarse. Furthermore, this old method was objectionable because of the loss of natural oils and the consequent loss of flavor. . . ." The Sears, Roebuck & Company catalog, 1935-1936, said: "Food nut chopper New! Chops nuts and raisins. Hopper and wood knob enameled in green or ivory with attractive decoration. Glass base. 39¢."

An unmarked nut chopper with red metal top, metal crank, clear glass base, and measuring 6" high × 3½" wide carries this label: "Nut Meat Container—Chopper —Dispenser. Put nut meats into glass jar. To use remove cap, invert jar and turn handle. Nut meats are chopped and dispensed in same operation; can be sprinkled into dish or into food. Unused nut meats can be kept in jar. FEDERAL."

Another unmarked chopper with orange metal top, clear glass base, and metal crank has A on the bottom. It measures 3¾" × 2⅛".

Also unmarked, with red metal lid, red wooden knob on crank, and clear glass base is a slightly taller chopper measuring 6⅛" × 2⅛".

FEDERAL TOOL CORP. CHICAGO A4 marks the bottom of the glass jar of a nut chopper with red plastic top and graduated marks from 1 teaspoon to 2 tablespoons. It has a metal crank and measures 7½" high and 2⅛" in diameter.

Rotary Mincers

A rotary mincer is a rolling device used to finely chop parsley, meats, and other vegetables and fruits. It is also used to cut noodles.

Similar to Fig. 104 is a mincer labeled GERMANY. It has a green wooden handle and ferrule and measures 7⅞" × 3". Another unmarked mincer with green wooden handle and ferrule measures 7⅜" × 3⅛".

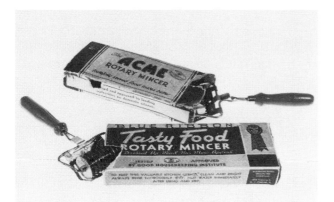

105. This rotary mincer marked Acme (top) has a green wooden handle and ferrule, and it measures 7³/₄" × 3¹/₈". Boxed: **$3.00—8.50**

Stated on the box is: *The Acme rotary mincer tastefully served food tastes better. Tested and Approved by Good Housekeeping Institute,* ©1932 *A.M.G.M. CO. Directions: To mince parsley, spinach, cabbage, celery, onions, fruits, etc., spread evenly on a chopping board a fair quantity of the food to be cut and press firmly upon the mincer while rolling it crosswise and lengthwise. Vegetables for relishes and salads can be chopped with lightning rapidity by this method.*

• *To Cut Noodles: Roll dough out flat and run mincer firmly across, cutting ten strips of uniform width at each stroke. Cooked chicken for chow mein or salads should be cut in the same manner.*

• *This utensil is especially valuable for preparing food for invalids and health food vegetables which are eaten raw.*

• *Important: Always use this utensil on a wooden chopping board and keep the guard snapped in place.*

Cleaning Directions: see side of carton. This utensil is not stainless. To keep it looking clean and bright, however, always rinse the metal parts with hot water **immediately after using.** *Place it over a hot stove to dry the moisture which remains between the cutting wheels. Tested and approved by leading authorities on domestic science.*

Acme wrote the following talk which was used by a firm who gave product demonstrations of the Acme rotary mincer.

Folks this cutter has just been introduced. It is called the rotary mincer and noodle cutter.

When you're making homemade noodles, you know how hard it is to cut them in even strips . . . notice how easy I do it. Imagine, I have the dough rolled out on this board. Dip the cutter into the flour, roll it across like this, and there you have ten even strips before you can say 'Jack Robinson.'

Some people when they chop nuts with a knife practically chop their finger off, besides letting them fly all over the place. When you want nuts chopped for cakes or salads just roll the mincer over them crisscross like this.

Cooking meats, chicken for chow mein, clams for chowder, this cut slices them into strips or small pieces, either way you want them.

When you put parsley through a grinder it gets too fine. This mincer, instead of crushing the parsley, cuts it quickly, clean, and dry leaving every bit of flavor and juice.

Cuts up your figs, dates, prunes, for salad and cakes. Cuts celery for soups and salads. Cuts up your vegetables for chow-chow relish.

Tenderizing steaks. Run this cutter over the meat crisscross to break the tough meat fibers.

To clean just press the button to open . . . like this. Rinse under hot water, shake off and hang up to dry.

The secret of using the rotary mincer is to rest the thumb on the catch where it is stamped "Press Thumb Here." Some demonstrators mention this in their demonstration, for it assures the user applying pressure while using the mincer.

Take shredded cabbage and mince it. Then add a few strips of carrots and beets and mince them in. It makes a colorful and attractive display and it can be used as a basis for a "spiel" on health giving advantages of salads and other vegetables and fruits.

The other mincer by Manufactured Specialities Company has a green wooden handle and is 7¹/₂" × 3¹/₈". The box said, *BLUE RIBBON TASTY FOOD MINCER*™ *Award of Merit, 1933. "Dressed Up Meal Has More Appeal." Tested and approved by Good Housekeeping Institute* (on front of box). *To keep this valuable kitchen utensil clean and bright always rinse thoroughly with hot water immediately after using and dry.*

Directions and Suggestions for Use: The usefulness of this invaluable time-saver is internationally known and needs little explanation. It is unequalled for making uniform home made noodles, for slicing the white meat of poultry, for chicken a la king, chow mein, salads, etc. Minces with lightning rapidity parsley, spinach, cabbage, onions, meats, nuts and all other vegetables. Spread evenly on a cutting board a quantity of the food to be cut and run mincer cross-wise and lengthwise. For chopping almonds, etc. first cut almonds.

To clean, rinse thoroughly with hot water under faucet immediately after using (on back of box).

Guarantee: The Tasty Food Rotary Mincer™ *has been given the approval of the Good Housekeeping Institute. We also unconditionally guarantee that this mincer has been examined before leaving our factory and will give absolute satisfaction. If, because of defective workmanship, this utensil does not meet with entire approval, it will be exchanged without cost, upon receipt of mincer and 25¢ for remailing charges* (on the other side of box).

Cutting Tools
(Other Than Knives)

A baller, ball cutter, or fruit and vegetable scoop is used to scoop out balls of fruits or vegetables for salads and fancy dishes. They sold for nine cents in 1936.

Similar to Fig. 106 is an A & J double ended tool with red wooden handle. It is also 7⅝" long. Six other sizes of colored handled baller-corers are owned by this collector.

A white wooden handle with metal ferrule, baller-corer 8⅞" long.

A single scoop with green wooden handle and metal ferrule, 4⅜" long, and another single scoop with green wooden handle which measures 5⅝" in length.

An unmarked, single scoop tool with green wooden handle, probably a Kitcheneed product, is 5½" long.

Another unmarked, single scoop tool with green wooden handle is 5¾". It probably was manufactured by Acme.

An unmarked, double-ended tool with a green wooden handle measures 7⅝".

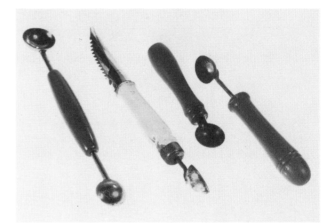

106. A & J-made, double ended baller (left) with green wooden handle was produced c. 1936. It is 7⅝" long. Unmarked baller-corer (left center) has a white wooden handle with metal ferrule and is 8⅞" long. Unmarked scoop (right center) has a green wooden handle with metal ferrule and is 4⅜" long. Another unmarked scoop (right) has a green wooden handle and is 5⅝" long. **$1.00—6.00**

Butter Curlers

Better Homes & Gardens, in April, 1932, said this about butter shells: "Dip the butter-shaper into boiling water for a half minute. Then draw it lightly over a piece of butter and drop the little roll into a bowl of cold or iced water. Butter shells are slightly oval in shape, and the outside is daintily grooved by the serrated edges of the shaper. With a little practice, a number of interesting shapes can be produced."

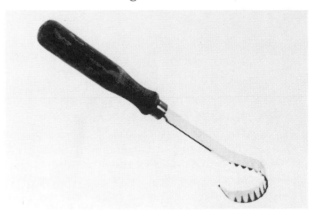

107. This butter curler is marked stainless on one side and Germany on the other. It has a green wooden handle and 4⅛" blade. Length is 8¼". **$1.00—3.50**

108. An A & J corer (left) has a green wooden handle and 3⅜" blade. Length is 6½".

Another A & J corer (second from left) has a green wooden handle with ivory band and tip. Stainless steel blade is 3⅜".

An EKCO Eterna™ corer (left center) has natural wooden handle with ivory tip and red and ivory bands, hang-up hole, 3⅜" blade of stainless steel, and length of 6⅝". It was made for F. W. Woolworth Company.

Androck made this 7⅛" stainless steel corer (right center) with a red teardrop handle and 3½" blade.

The Vaughan Novelty Manufacturing Company made this corer (second from right) with green wooden handle, ferrule, and 3½" blade. It is 6¼" long.

Stainless steel corer (right) has a blue wooden handle, 3⅛" blade and length of 6¼".

Unmarked: **$1.00–2.50**
Marked: **Higher price**

Corers and Parers

A corer is used to remove fruit cores with a twisting motion. Apple corers and parers are used for peeling, coring, and scraping fruits and vegetables. The point is used to remove eyes from potatoes and pineapples; sawtooth blade is for scaling fish. The October, 1929, issue of *House Beautiful* said, "When preserving or making applesauce, a fruit parer will be a real joy. It obviates hacking up and therefore wasting fruit, and therefore saves money."

Not illustrated, but similar to Fig. 108,

are four other green-handled corer-parers, unmarked, ranging in size from 6⅜" to 6⅞" long.

An unmarked, green wooden handled tool, probably by Acme, is 6⅞" long with a 3½" blade.

Another unmarked, green wooden handled tool has a ferrule, 2⅝" blade, and 6⅜" length.

An unmarked, green wooden handled tool, probably by Kitcheneed, measures 6⅞" with 3⅜" blade.

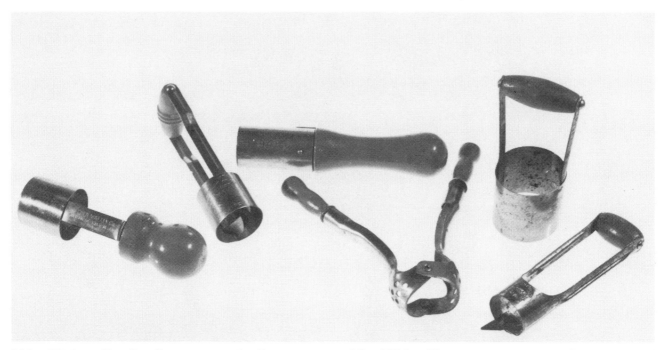

109. Kitchen Novelty Company made the corer (left) with a green wooden handle. Called the Perfect Corer, it is 4⅞″× 1¼″.

Stomar made a stainless steel corer (second from left) with a horizontal, green wooden handle. It is 4¾″× 1½″.   **$1.50–3.50**

✂ The Durabilt grapefruit corer (top center) has a green wooden handle and is 5⅝″× 1⅛″.
                                                $2.50–4.50

Corer (bottom center), patented March 29, 1927, has a green wooden handle and a perforated bowl. It is 5¼″× 1½″.   **$3.00–8.50**

It was filed as patent number 1,622,874 on August 18, 1926. The inventor was John Kovat of Bridgeport, Conn., assignor to Lorraine Metal Manufacturing Company of Bridgeport, Connecticut.

Stainless steel grapefruit corer (second from right) has a horizontal, green wooden handle and is 4¾″× 1¾″. Patent number 1,568,008 was filed on May 9, 1925 and patented December 29, 1925. Cecil C. Thomas of Takoma Park, Maryland, the inventor, called it an implement for removing cores from citrus fruits.   **$1.50–3.00**

The HI-SPEED™ corer (right) has a red wooden handle and is 4⅜″× 1″.   **$1.50–3.00**

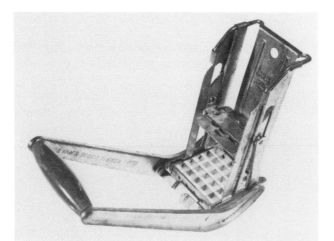

110. EKCO Tomado Holland French fry cutter is made of heavily blocked tin and has a red wooden handle, c. 1950. This was manufactured in Holland for several years before EKCO made it in the U.S. It is 9¾″× 3⅝″.   **$1.50–6.00**

✂ Grapefruit Corers

Similar to Fig. 109 is a Wizard stainless steel tool with red wooden handle. It is 5″ × 1¼″.

French Fry Cutters

French fry cutters cleverly divided a potato into familiar french fry shapes in one motion. To use: lift up handle, put in potato, and push down slowly on handle.

Similar to Fig. 110 is an EKCO french fry cutter with green wooden handle. It is 9¾″ × 3½″.

The VILLA™ potato chipper, patent number 490250 and register number 189275 was made in England. It has a green wooden handle and is 9¾″ × 3½″.

111. Unmarked 5⅞″ fruit pitter (left) has a green wooden handle and a 1¾″ blade. **$1.25—3.50**

Though unmarked, this garnisher (center) is probably by Acme. It has a green wooden handle, 3″ blade and measures 6¾″. Unmarked garnisher with a vertical, white wooden handle and ferrule has a 3⅜″ blade and measures 5½″. **$1.50—6.00**

Fruit Pitters

These were used to remove pits from fruits or to core tomatoes.

Garnishers

A garnisher is a corrugated vegetable knife used to make fancy cuts.

Similar to Fig. 111 is an unmarked, green wooden handled tool, probably by Kitcheneed. It is 7¼″ long with a 3⅜″ blade.

An unmarked tool with vertical, green wooden handle and a ferrule has a length of 5¾″ and a 3¼″ blade.

An unmarked tool with a light green wooden handle is 6⅝″ with a 3¼″ blade.

Another unmarked tool with a green wooden handle is 6½″ with a 3″ blade.

An unmarked tool with a red wooden handle is 6⅝″ with a 3″ blade.

The following is a demonstration talk on the Acme Metal Goods Manufacturing Company garnishing knife.

"The first cutter I am going to show you is known as the 'garnishing knife.' It makes those crispy 'krinkle' cut French fries. To make these fancy French fry potatoes, cut into thick slices, pile them one on top of the other and crosscut them like this . . . then you have three times the browning surface.

The next time you want to serve French fries: cut them this way, place them in ice water for about half an hour, drain them and put them into hot shortening until they are

(continued)

112. The box describes the set as follows: *The Acme garnishing set—tastefully served food tastes better C 1932 A.M.&M. CO. (appears on front of box). Only a few of the various ways of using this set are described. Daily use will suggest new and time-saving means of quickly preparing many delicious and attractive dishes. It assures successful and tastefully served meals. Acme Metal Goods Manufacturing Company, Newark, N.J., U.S.A. (on side). To keep these utensils looking clean and bright* **always** *rinse with hot water and dry thoroughly* **immediately after using**. *Do not soak them in water. To sharpen: Use a small half round file (on other side).*

Parer & corer. *To peel potatoes, fruits, etc., use the small opening at the bottom, as illustrated. Coring apples: Insert thru apple and turn. Use the serrated edge for scaling fish and the point for removing eyes of pineapples, potatoes, crimping pies, etc.*

Ball cutter. *In making potato balls, butter balls, etc., place the edge of the ball cutter toward potato and turn with a circular motion as shown, cutting out pieces of spherical shape. Can be used on fruit such as watermelon, cantaloupe, etc.*

Garnisher. *To cut fancy french fried potatoes: Cut several slices with the garnisher, pile together, then cut them lengthways. To cut lattice potatoes: Cut thru potatoes as illustrated, turn quarter way around and cut thru edge. This also can be done with carrots, beets, apples, etc. to improve appearance of halved grapefruits, etc., trim edge of rind with garnisher.*

Vegetable slicer. *To slice vegetables, cold slaw, etc., adjust slide to desired size, cutting toward you. Slice potatoes with same cutter (on back of box). Price $1.00, Made in U.S.A. (on end of box).*

The Acme tools are unmarked and have 3½″ green wooden handles. The corer is 6⅞″ with 3⅜″ blade. The garnisher is 6¾″ with a 3″ blade. The slicer has a thumb rest and is 6½″ with a 2¼″ blade. The ball cutter is 5¾″ with a 2¼″ blade. **$6.50—9.50**

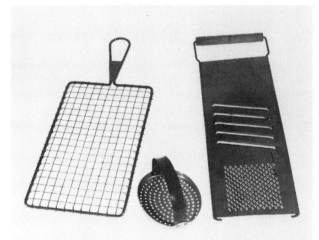

113. Grater (left), marked ACME THE ONLY GENUINE SAFETY GRATER, has a green metal handle and is 13⅛″×5⅜″. **$1.50—6.50**

An unmarked flat oval grater or fish scaler (center) is probably by Aluminum Goods Manufacturing Company. It has a green metal handle and is 4⅛″× 3⅛″. **$1.00—3.00**

An unmarked metal grater and slicer (right) has a horizontal, green wooden handle and is 13″×4½″. **$1.50—4.50**

114. Climax rotary grater (left) has a green metal bracket and green metal crank with natural wooden handle, c. 1935. It is 10½″×4″. **$5.00—9.00**

A grater by Lorraine Metal Manufacturing Company (right) has a green metal bracket and green wooden handle, c. 1935. It is 8½″×2⅜″. **$8.00—15.00**

115. An ice cream scoop marked Roberts—Japan on the finger rest (right) has a red wooden handle and metal scoop. It is 8½″×2½″.

An unmarked scoop (left) has a green wooden handle. Blade in scoop is rotated by turning wing-nut to remove ice cream. It is 7¼″×2⅜″. **$2.00—15.00**

golden brown . . . you'll say they are the most delicious French fries you ever tasted.

For something different, try the 'lattice' or 'waffle' cut. To make the waffle cut . . . you cut thin slices . . . cut and turn . . . cut and turn. That gives you the lattice effect. For pickled beets, cut them this way . . . they'll taste twice as good.

When you serve grapefruit or oranges, trim the rind like this. Cut your apples, pineapple slices, and other fruits for salads with this cutter. Use it for cutting dainty butter or margarine squares, sandwich or brick ice cream.

Everything you cut with this must come out fancy. It's fantastic for hors d'oeurves, sandwiches, cheese, carrots, hard boiled eggs, bananas, or what have you."

Graters

Two types of graters are hand and rotary. A hand grater is an implement that has a rough surface or sharp-edged slits or jagged holes on which to shred or grate foods. A rotary grater is used to grate fine, medium or coarse bread crumbs, chocolate, nutmeg, raw vegetables, and cheese.

Similar to Fig. 114 is a grater with green wooden handle and a metal bracket. It is 8½″ × 2⅜″. A "5" appears on the inside opposite clamp.

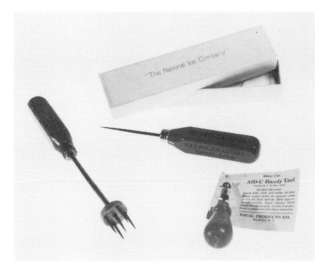

116. A Chip-Chop™ ice pick (left) by Apex Products Corporation has a green wooden handle and is 9³/₈″ with ⁷/₈″ points. Directions on the pick say, "Place cube in glass. Rest points on cube and tap handle sharply. Place only one cube in glass at a time." On the other sides of pick are recipes for a Manhattan, dry martini, old fashioned, Tom Collins, Bronx, and orange blossom drinks.

National Ice Company pick (center) is marked: "Refrigeration Canal 2463; Ice 1358 Canal 2423; Coal-Coke 2371." It has a four-sided, red wooden handle and is 7″ long with a 2⁷/₈″ pick.

An unmarked, flat pointed pick with a green wooden handle (right) is 3³/₈″ long with a 1¹/₄″ pick. The display card reads: *Many uses/Aid-U handy tool, patent & trademark registration pending. See that flat point. Opens milk, juice, and edible oil cans. Easily makes holes on opposite sides of top for fluid and air. Milk caps removed quickly. Paper staples lifted neatly. Handy ice pick scriber. Punches holes in paper and thin sheet materials. Ideal Products Company, Brooklyn, N.Y.*

Marked: **$2.00—4.00**
Unmarked: **$1.00—3.00**

Ice Picks

The needle-sharp pick is used to reduce the size of a solid block of ice to manageable chips. The wooden handle with a weighted metal cap is used for crushing ice.

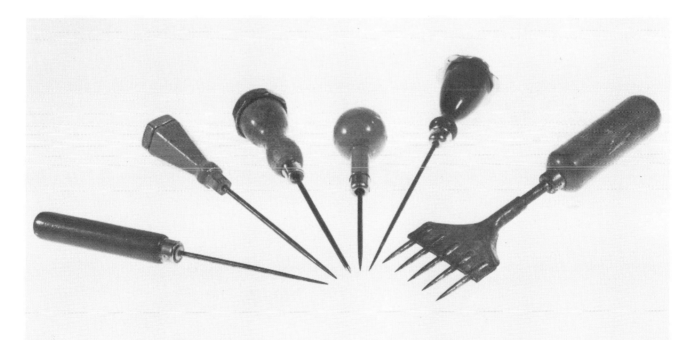

117. A Household Specialties pick (left) has a red wooden handle and ferrule. It measures 8³/₄″ with a 4¹/₂″ pick.

An unmarked 8³/₈″ pick (second from left) has a six-sided, green wooden handle, metal cap and 4⁷/₈″ pick.

Another unmarked 7⁵/₈″ pick (left center) has a green wooden handle, eight-sided metal cap and a 3⁷/₈″ pick.

An unmarked 6″ pick (right center) with a green wooden sphere on the end with one flat side has a 2⁷/₈″ pick.

One unmarked 8³/₈″ tool (second from right) has a red wooden handle, six-sided metal cap and a 4³/₄″ pick.

The unmarked ice chipper (right) has a green wooden handle and a 3¹/₂″ × 4⁵/₈″ pick. Overall length is 8³/₄″.

Marked: **$3.00—6.00**
Unmarked: **$2.00—4.00**

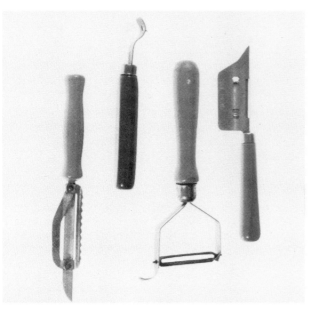

Parer-Peelers

This tool is used to remove skin from vegetables or fruits.

Slicers

Cheese slicers have been made in many styles, but most feature a strong, taut wire which cuts the cheese in even slices.

Vegetable slicers are used to slice various vegetables and often have adjustable blades.

Similar to Fig. 119 is an unmarked vegetable slicer with a green wooden handle. Length is 6¼″ and blade is 2⅛″.

An unmarked vegetable slicer with a white wooden handle, ferrule and thumb rest is 6⅜″ long with a 2⅛″ blade.

118. A tool with a green wooden handle (left) is possibly used for scoring and cutting cucumbers or paring and removing eyes from potatoes. Length is 6⅜″ and blade is 3⅜″. **$1.25–3.50**
An orange peeler by Ocko (left center) has a protruding point to peel oranges, a 5″ length, and a 1⅜″ blade.
A vegetable parer (right center) by Yates Manufacturing Company has a green wooden handle, 2⅝″ blade, and 6⅜″ length.
A parer with replaceable razor blade (right) has a green wooden handle, 2¾″ blade and 6⅛″ length.

120. An unmarked slicer with a green wooden handle, 4½″ serrated blade, horizontal metal bar, and a length of 8⅛″. **$1.25–3.50**

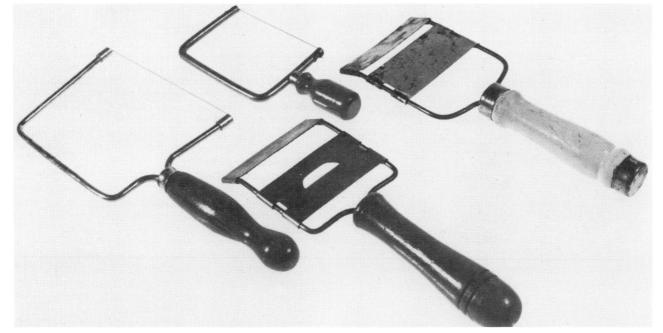

119. Unmarked slicer (left) with red wooden handle measures 7¾″ with 4″ wire. **$1.00–6.00**
This unmarked cheese slicer (top) has a green wooden handle, 2⅞″ wire, and 4½″ length. It was given as a premium for Kraft Velveeta cheese. **$1.00–6.00**
Unmarked vegetable slicer (bottom center), prob-

ably by Acme Metal Goods Manufacturing Company, c. 1932, has a green wooden handle, thumb rest, 2⅜″ blade, and length of 6½″. **$1.25–3.50**
Unmarked vegetable slicer (right) has a white wooden handle, ferrule and metal tip. Blade is 2¼″ and length is 6¾″. **$1.25–3.50**

121. EKCO tomato slicer (top) made in Tomado, Holland, sold for fifty-nine cents. It has a red wooden handle, ferrule, ten blades that measure 5⅞"×3⅜", and a length of 10¼". The package gives instructions in German, English, and French. The EKCO slicers made in Holland are older than those made in the U.S. **$1.00—4.50**

Another EKCO slicer (left) has a four-sided, red wooden handle with a hang-up hole; ferrule; ten blades measuring 5¾"×3½", and a length of 11¼". On the package is found: *EKCO Miracle Tomato Slicer price 59¢. Tomatoes-cucumbers-eggs-carrots-cheese-butter* (on front) *Slices thin-Slices even-Slices quick-Slices easy.* No. T-6321P.

HOW TO USE. Wash and dry tomatoes. Hold the slicer in the right hand, saw-edge uppermost. Put a dish or plate under the slicer. Take a firm tomato, and move it gently backwards and forwards along the slicer. When it cannot be cut any further, hold the slices from underneath, and continue the sawing movement until they are cut through. With an EKCO Tomato Slicer a whole tomato can be easily cut into thin, even slices. No. 54432.

$1.00—4.50

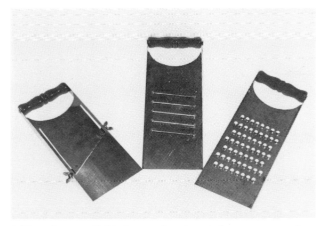

122. Grater (left) has a horizontal, green wooden handle and wing nuts to adjust the blade. It is 10"×4". **$1.50—3.25**

Simplex™ grater has a horizontal, red wooden handle and five fixed blades. It is 10⅞"×4". **$1.50—4.50**

This Simplex™ shredder (right) made by Remark Manufacturing Company has a horizontal, green wooden handle. It is 10⅞"×4⅛". **$1.50—4.50**

123. The package for this vegetable knife set reads: *Kitcheneed Vegetable Knife Set tested and approved by Good Housekeeping Institute.* Instructions for use read as follows:

Peeler and Corer

To peel potatoes, apples, pears, and other vegetables and fruits with a peeler, place the slotted edge against the article to be peeled, and draw toward you. To core apples and other fruits, send the point of the corer through the fruit and make a complete twisting turn, then withdraw. Use the toothedge of the peeler to scale fish, and the point for removing eyes from potatoes or pineapples.

Ball Cutter

To cut balls out of butter, potatoes, melons, pineapples, and other fruits, place the cutting edge firmly against the object and turn with a scooping motion.

Garnisher

For French fried potatoes, cut several slices of potatoes, pile them together and cut them lengthwise. For lattice potatoes, cut potatoes as pictured, turn slices quarter way around and cut through edge. Can also be used for carrots, beets, apples, etc., and to decorate edges of oranges or grapefruit.

Vegetable Slicer

First adjust the blade to the thickness of the slice desired. . . . Then by a drawing motion, toward you, potatoes, carrots, cucumbers, and many other kinds of vegetables can be quickly and uniformly sliced. There is nothing to compare with it for slicing cole slaw or potatoes.

We guarantee this set of knives to give you complete satisfaction and to be perfect in every respect. If, because of any defect in workmanship, these knives do not meet with your approval return this set to us with 25¢ for refund.

Kitcheneed Products Co. Buffalo, New York, Fort Erie, Canada, Vegetable Knife Set tested and approved by Good Housekeeping Institute. To keep these knives clean and bright always rinse them in hot water after using, and dry them thoroughly. Use a small half-round file to keep the edge of the knives sharp, and in the best of working condition.

$6.50—9.50

Juicers

Orange juice became popular in America in the 1920s because refrigerated boxcars made fruits more readily available. Citrus growers promoted their fruits through advertising campaigns. Because Americans preferred oranges in juice form, many kinds of juice extractors that minimized time and effort came on the market.

Lever juicers are so named because juice is extracted from a cut orange by pressing on the lever.

Rotary juicers were operated by turning a crank to extract juice. The Kwickway Juicer, Fig. 125, was invented by C. E. Elliot and patented on January 14, 1930. It "relates to

juice extractors and for extracting juices from oranges, lemons, citrus, and other fruits and provides complete extraction of the juices with facility and extreme rapidity and to separate the seed and pulp to obtain the juice in its purest quality . . ." Elliot stated in the patent application.

124. Juice-O-mat™ with Tilt-Top™ (right) is made by Rival Manufacturing Company, patent numbers D-151103; 2,394,763; 2,142,975, and other patents pending. Catalog number is NJ-848. The juicer has a chrome and metal top and red metal base. It is 7⅞″ × 6½″ × 5¾″.
$4.00—7.00
The Orange Flow™ juicer (right) was made by Chicago Die Casting Manufacturing Company, patent number 101,957, and patented on November 17, 1936. It is green metal and is 8½″ × 7¼″ × 6¼″. **$4.00—9.00**

125.   The Speedo Super Juicer™ (left) was made by Central States Manufacturing Company. It has a rotating metal reamer, strainer, cup with pour spout, bracket to hang on wall, and red wooden knob. It is 5¼″ × 4¾″.   **$3.50–9.00**

American Home, in 1932, called it, *A smoothly running efficient device with a generous capacity. Price is $1.75, Central States.* The George Worthington Company said this about it in 1936: *Perforated strainer holds back seeds, pulp and pith; only clear juice is delivered. Slips easily into wall bracket. . . .*

Kwikway Products, Inc. made this juicer (right), patent number 1,743,661. The juicer has a green wooden knob and is 6½″ × 4″. Directions for operation are on handle and crank. The display tag says: *One-year Guarantee paper: Instructions for using the new KWIKWAY Orange Juicer and Grapefruit Juicer. For best results, follow these directions. Important: do not apply pressure with the left hand; but let the simple turning of the crank, with the right hand do all the work.*

1. *Cut the fruit as nearly exactly in half as possible.*
2. *Lift the upper cup of the Juicer, and place half of the fruit (face down) over the crossed wire dome in the lower cup, applying only enough pressure to prevent its falling off.*
3. *Close the upper cup, covering the fruit, and without applying any pressure with either hand, start turning the crank . . . slowly at first, and then with increasing speed . . . and with slightly increasing pressure with the right hand only.*
4. *As the turning progresses, increase the pressure with both hands, until the lessened resistance indicates the completion of the juice process.*
5. *Without lifting the upper cup, pour the juice out of one lip in the lower cup, and then the other . . . alternating until all the juice has been delivered.*
6. *Lift the upper cup, remove the hull of the fruit, replace with the other half, and repeat the process.*
7. *To clean, let the cold water run into the lower bowl, shake thoroughly, pour water out, and allow to dry. The Kwikway Juicers will not rust or stain. In juicing lemons, cut the tip off the fruit before inserting in juicer. Kwikway Juicers are tested and approved by Good Housekeeping Institute and fully guaranteed by Kwikway Products, Inc., St. Louis, U.S.A.*

126. The Universal fruit juice extractor by Landers, Frary & Clark (left) is a metal juice reamer on a green metal, four-legged stand. It has a black wooden knob and is 10″×5¾″. **$3.50–10.00**
Handy Andy™ juice extractor (right) was made by H. A. Specialty Company, Inc., patent number 2,008,899. It has a green metal base and crank bracket and a black wooden knob. The pitcher and reamer are not shown. Juicer is 10½″×7″. This juicer was invented by Charles Dawn, New York, N.Y., who filed it on May 23, 1930 and patented it July 23, 1935. The Sears, Roebuck Company catalog, in 1935, ran this listing: *Place half an orange or*

lemon in the aluminum cup . . . turn the handle. Lipped green glass pitcher. Extractor quickly taken apart for cleaning. $1.25 value . . . $1.00. In 1931, *American Home* said: *The Handy Andy juice extractor above is a combination reamer and pitcher. After the fruit juice has been crushed and strained through to the pitcher leaving seed and pulp on the reamer, just remove pitcher and serve. Price $1.67 postpaid. Handy Andy Specialty Co., Inc., 534 Van Alst Avenue, Long Island City, N.Y.*
Complete: **$15.00–22.00**
Reamer and pitcher missing: **$1.50–7.00**

Knives and Knife Sharpeners

In 1928 the Good Housekeeping Institute said a basic set of kitchen cutlery might include a grapefruit knife, two paring knives, a case knife for spreading toast or sandwiches, a general utility or boning knife, a slicer, a carver, one narrow spatula, one broad spatula, two forks, and a serrated bread knife.

To aid in keeping knives sharp and usable, every set of knives was to be accompanied by a satisfactory knife sharpener. Knives were easily kept sharp and in good condition if they were properly stored when not in use. Some type of knife rack was the most convenient way to store knives, because they could be easily reached, the blades were protected, and the danger of cutting fingers was lessened.

If knives were made of carbon steel which rusted and discolored, they had to be rubbed with a cork and scouring powder or steel wool to brighten them. A wash and rinse was all that was necessary for stainless steel blades. Colored enamel or lacquer finished handles could not be left to soak nor washed in a dishwashing machine because even the best of finishes was apt to chip and break off, leaving the knives unsightly.

Bread Knives

When bread is fresh, it can be cut more easily and with much less crumbling with a bread knife having a serrated edge. If other knives are used for cutting bread, they soon lose their keen edge.

Cake and Pie Server

These are used to cut and serve portions.

Similar to Fig. 128 is the Rumford slotted pie server with stained green wooden handle and 4½″ blade. Length is 8¼″. The

127. Clyde G™, tested and approved by Good Housekeeping Institute, The Clyde Cutlery Company, is written on the side of this knife (top). Compliments of the Smith Bros. Hardware Company, 1930, is on the other side of this knife with 9″ blade and green wooden handle.

Smith Brothers Hardware Company of Columbus, Ohio, has been in business for over 100 years. They are a wholesale distributor of hardware and industrial tools which they sell all over Ohio and parts of adjoining states. Mr. Leo Hall, president, said that Clyde Cutlery must have personalized this cutlery as an advertisement to be given out by Smith Brothers Hardware salesmen because Smith Brothers would not have picked one of several thousand products to put their name on for a giveaway. Marked: **up to $8.00**

The Samson Never Crumb Bread Knife™ (second from top) is genuine stainless, has a green wooden handle and is 12⅛″ with a 7¾″ blade. Another knife with a green wooden handle (third) is marked made in U.S.A. and measures 12¾″ with a 8¼″ blade.

An unmarked knife (fourth) has a green wooden handle, curved 8⅞″ blade, and length of 13⅜″.

An unmarked knife (fifth) measuring 12¾″ has a green wooden handle and 8½″ blade.

Another unmarked knife (bottom) has a four-sided, green wooden handle and 8¼″ blade. It is 12¾″ long. **$2.00–3.50**

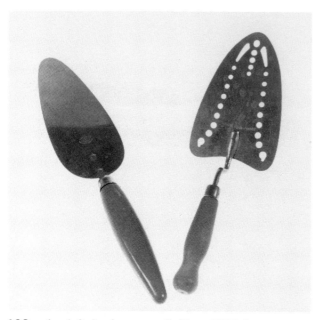

128.   An A & J cake server (left), c. 1936, has a green wooden handle and 5⅞" blade. Length is 10⅝".

A 9" pie server (right) was marked Rumford, the Wholesome Baking Powder. It is perforated, has a stained green wooden handle, and 4½" blade.
$2.00—3.50

Rumford Chemical Works, Rumford, Rhode Island, offered cooking utensils as premiums during various years from 1900 to 1930. The dates and the manufacturers of these premiums are unavailable. The Rumford Company, as it is now known, came under its present ownership in 1950. The office and plant were moved to Terre Haute, Indiana, in 1966.

Fruit Knives

These are used to cut the meat out of fruit.

Paring Knives

These are used to remove skin from fruits and vegetables.

Spatulas

These are used to remove batter from a bowl, loosen cakes from baking pans, and spread frosting.

Similar to Fig. 130 is a tool with a green teardrop handle, probably by Androck, which measures 11¾" and has a 7" blade.

129.   A Geneva stainless grapefruit knife (left) has a green wooden handle with ivory band and 3¼" blade. Length is 6¾".

A stainless steel fruit knife (second from left) has a green wooden handle, 3⅜" blade and length of 7¼".

A stainless steel paring knife (left center) has green wooden handle, 3" blade, and measures 6⅜".

A 6¼" Quikut™ stainless knife (right center) has a round, green wooden handle and 2½" blade.

Another Quikut knife (second from right) has a four-sided, green wooden handle, 2⅝" blade and a length of 6⅜".

A knife with D. Harrington & Sons, stainless marked on the blade (right) measures 6⅝" with a 3" blade. The green wooden handle is marked Good Housekeeping Shop on one side and Frigidaire on the other.
$1.00—3.50

Another unmarked tool with a green wooden handle is 11¾″ long with a 7″ blade.

An unmarked tool with a red wooden handle with ivory band and tip is 11¾″ and has a 7″ blade. It came from Woolworth's.

A tool with a green wooden handle with ivory band is 11⅜″ × 7⅛″.

Utility Knives

They are used when a paring knife is too short, such as for cutting a grapefruit in half. They can also be used to slice meat or cakes.

Knife Sharpeners

There were several small household sharpeners of simple design, c. 1928, which were easy to use and did not require the skill older methods demanded.

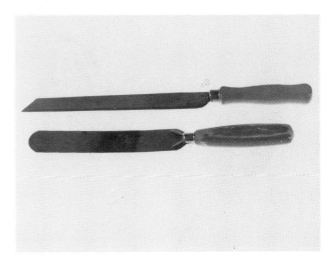

130. A Samson stainless steel spatula (bottom) has a green wooden handle, 7″ blade, and measures 11¾″.

An unmarked 12⅞″ utility knife has a green wooden handle and 8⅜″ blade. **$1.00–3.50**

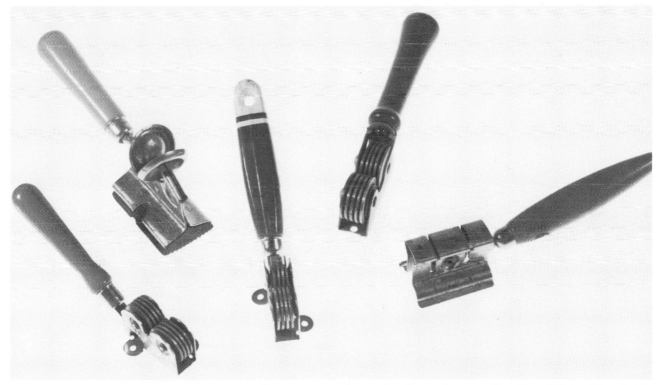

131. An A & J rotary knife sharpener (left) has a green wooden handle, c. 1936. It is 5¾″ with a 1⅞″ sharpener. A rotary sharpener marked EKCO and A & J (center) has a red wooden handle with hang-up hole and ivory tip and band. This handle was made exclusively for F. W. Woolworth Company, c. 1949. It has a raised ridge in the center of the handle. Length is 6¾″ with a 1⅞″ sharpener. A & J also made a rotary sharpener (right) with a four-sided, green wooden handle. Directions to *draw knife thru here and here* are marked on top the 2″ sharpener. Length is 7⅛″.

A sharpener by Ace Manufacturing Corporation, patent number 1,566,140, (right center) has a non-ferruled red wooden handle. It is 6¾″ with a 2⅝″ sharpener. This was invented by George Jones of Philadelphia, Pa., who filed it on April 4, 1925 and patented it on December 15, 1925.

Edlund Sure Sharp™ #3 (left center) has a green wooden handle with black rubber grid on the base, patent number 1,990,117. It is 7⅛″ with a 2⅝″ sharpener. Directions say, *Hold sharpener in left hand. Draw knife toward you, keeping it straight and level. Caution—place sharpener near edge of table or shelf. Use a firm stroke, but not too heavy pressure.* This was invented by H. J. Edlund who filed it on January 26, 1934, and patented it February 2, 1935. **$2.00–10.00**

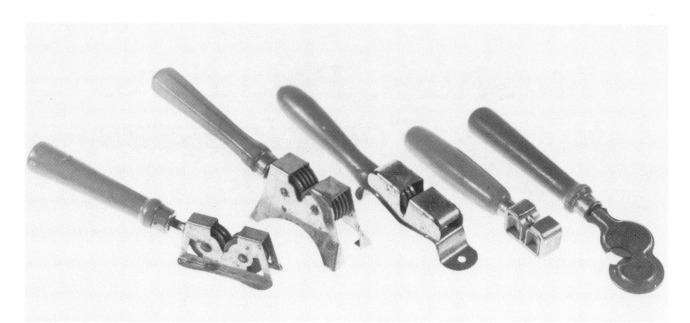

132. An Eversharp™ sharpener (left) has a green wooden handle, 2³/₈" sharpener, and length of 6¹/₂".

Another Eversharp tool (left center), patent number DES. 82929, has an eight-sided, green wooden handle and 2¹/₂" sharpener. Length is 6³/₄".

A Presto™ knife sharpener (center) has a green wooden handle, 2¹/₂" sharpener, and 7¹/₈" length.

A sharpener marked Rotary patent 233,856

English made, has a green wooden handle, 1³/₈" sharpener, and length of 5¹/₈". The same sharpener with a blue wooden handle (not shown) was also made.

A Sharp-Ezy™ (right) by Samson has a green wooden handle, 2¹/₂" blade, and length of 7".

$2.00—10.00

Good Housekeeping magazine in December, 1930, said: "If regular attention is not given to the sharpening of the kitchen knives, the bread may be haggled, the vegetables peeled too thickly, even the Christmas bird mutilated. Nothing is more ruinous to the success of the Christmas dinner than a dull knife. A knife sharpener at hand, simple and easy to use, is the answer."

A stone is used to sharpen stainless steel knives without marring or scratching the finish. A bevel or crown in the center of the sharpening section permits the flat surface to come in contact with the knife edge.

A rod is an ideal sharpener for all household knives.

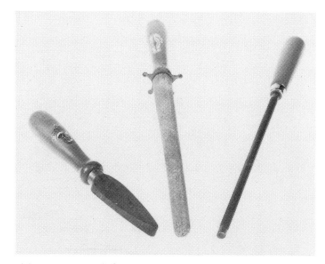

133. A stone (left) marked Carborundum, made in Niagara Falls, N.Y., has a green wooden handle and a 3" octagonal stone. Length is 7¹/₄".

A Norton Abrasives Quickcut™ knife sharpener (center) has a green wooden handle and measures 12⁷/₈", c. 1939. The W. Bingham Company, Cleveland, Ohio, said, *Norton abrasives sharpen household cutlery with Quickcut knife sharpener. Smooth clean slices, carving simple. An inexpensive but serviceable sharpener which cuts quickly and produces a sharp clean edge. Strengthened by a steel rod which extends it full length. Per dozen $2.40.* **$2.00—10.00**

An unmarked knurled steel rod with the tip missing (right) has a green wooden handle and measures 12¹/₄". **$1.50—4.50**

Mashers, Pounders, Ricers, Food Presses, Food Mills

Mashers are used to mash vegetables. They sold from ten cents to twenty cents each in 1935.

Similar to Fig. 134 is an unmarked masher with a green wooden handle and four loops. It is 9¼" × 4".

An unmarked masher with a green wooden handle with ivory tip and band, ferrule and five loops is 9¾" × 3⅞".

An unmarked masher with a green wooden handle with ivory band and four loops measures 9½" × 3½".

An unmarked masher having a white with blue tip wooden handle and five loops is 9¾" × 3⅞".

135. This A & J oval masher and ricer has a green wooden handle with ivory tip and band and a ferrule. It is 9½" × 4".   **$2.00–3.50**

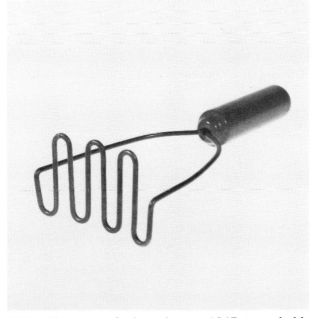

134. This unmarked masher, c. 1947, is probably by A & J. It has a green wooden handle, ferrule, five loops and measures 9½" × 3⅞".   **$2.00–3.50**

An unmarked masher with a ridged, red wooden handle, ferrule, and four loops is 9⅜" × 4".

An unmarked masher has a yellow with green band and tip wooden handle, ferrule and four loops measures 9¾" × 4⅛".

An unmarked masher with a red with ivory band wooden handle, made by A & J, has four loops and measures 9¾" × 4⅛".

Pounders

These are also known as beetles, meat frets, meat tenderizers, and steak mauls. They are used to make meat tender by pounding it.

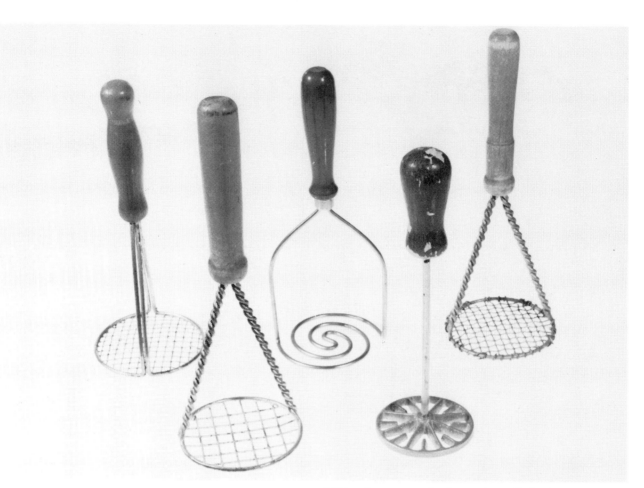

136. An unmarked masher (left) has a green wooden handle with ivory band, flat ¼″ wire mesh base, and double metal supports. It is 8⅝″ × 3⅝″.

An unmarked masher (right) with a green wooden handle with ivory band has a flat ½″ mesh base and twisted wire supports. It is 9⅝″ × 3½″.

An unmarked masher (center) with a red wooden handle has a flat series of circles for a base. It is 9⅛″ × 3⅛″.

Another unmarked masher (right center) with a red wooden handle has a flat wheel with spokes for a base. It is 8¼″ × 2¾″.

Another unmarked masher (left center) has a green wooden handle, flat ¼″ mesh base, and twisted wire supports. It is 9½″ × 3⅜″. **$2.00–3.50**

Similar to Fig. 137 is an unmarked tool with a green wooden handle. It is 11½″ × 2¼″.

137. This unmarked potato masher (standing) has a green wooden handle and wooden beetle. It is 10¾″ × 2⅛″.

Munising wooden meat fret has a green wooden handle and is 12⅜″ × 3⅜″. The partial label says it is carefully made from selected Michigan hardwood, Munising, Mich. **$2.00–5.00**

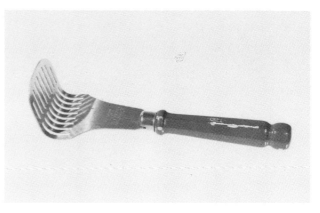

138. Meat tenderizer and ax (left) has the blade attached with a wing nut. The green wooden handled tool measures 10½″ with a 3⅛″ ax blade and a 2⅜″ tenderizer. It was patented December 5, 1922, by The Tyler Manufacturing Company.

Meat tenderizer and ax by Kristee Products Company (center) has a length of 8⅝″ with a 2¼″ ax blade and 2¼″ tenderizer. Shown with a green wooden handle, it was also available in red.

Meat pounder and tenderizer (right) has a green wooden handle and a length of 9″ with 2¼″ ax blade and 2″ tenderizer. Patent number is D 11330.
Metal: **$4.00–8.00**
Wood: **$1.50 7.00**

139. Samson potato ricer is stainless steel and has an eight-sided, green wooden handle. It is 9⅜″ × 2½″. **$2.00–5.00**

Similar to Fig. 138 is an unmarked meat tenderizer and ax with a green wooden handle and blade attached with wing nut. It is 10½″ with a 3⅛″ ax and 2⅜″ tenderizer.

Ricers

Potato ricers are used to mash or rice potatoes.

Similar to Fig. 139 is an Androck potato ricer with a green wooden handle with ball tip. It is 8⅝″ × 2½″.

Rotary ricers are used for making purees and soups, ricing potatoes, making grape juice, applesauce, and preparing baby food.

Similar to Fig. 140 is an unmarked tin colander with metal handle and wooden pestle with green wooden handle. Height is 9″; pestle is 10⅜″ long.

Food presses are also known as fruit presses or potato ricers. They peel and mash fruits and vegetables, pressing results in strings similar to rice. These sold for twenty-five cents in 1932 in the *Sears, Roebuck* catalog.

140. This unmarked ricer, c. 1930, has a tin colander, green wooden handle, and wood pestle with green wooden handle. It is 8⅞″ × 7¼″ with a 10⅜″ pestle. Colander and pestle: **$6.00–10.00**
Colander only: **$3.00–4.00**
Pestle only: **$1.50–2.50**

111

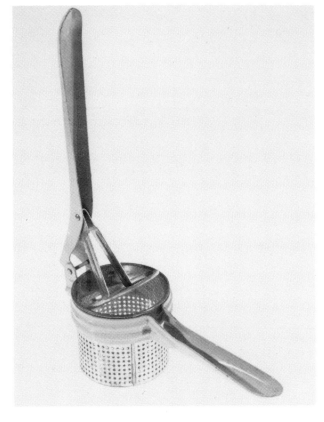

Similar to Fig. 141 is an unmarked press with apple green metal handles. It is 10¾" × 3".

Food Mills

These mash and strain vegetables and fruits for canning, freezing, and everyday preparation.

Similar to Fig. 142 is the Foley food mill, patent number 2,051,095. It has a red wooden handle and crank knob and measures 11½" × 5½".

141. A food press by Handy Things has light green metal handles and is 11" × 3¾". **$2.00—7.50**

142. A Foley food mill, patent number 1,921,936, has a green wooden handle and crank knob and was patented in 1933. Directions say, "To clean, remove thumb screw, lift out masher." In December, 1936, the George Worthington Company said of this food mill: *Family size: A speedy and efficient potato ricer. Will also grate crackers, cheese and nuts. 1½ quart capacity. Simple to use; easy to clean. Scraper with handle; removes food from bottom. Clamps hold mill firmly on slightly larger dish, bowl or kettle. Made of heavily tinned steel, rust proof.* **$3.50—8.50**

Measuring Tools

Exact measurements are important, according to 1925 and 1926 cookbooks. Every housewife should have a half-pint measuring cup. Many measuring cups held two to three tablespoons more than one-half pint. A druggist's graduated glass could always be relied upon if there was any doubt of exact measurement.

Spoon measurements had to be accurate. A set of spoons on a ring could be bought to measure exactly—a tablespoon, dessert spoon, teaspoon, half teaspoon, and quarter teaspoon.

How to Measure

Measurement should be level. Leveling could be accomplished with the flat side of a knife. Flour, powdered sugar, baking powder, and soda should be sifted before measuring. Butter, lard, or any hard fats should be packed down in the cup or spoon and leveled with a knife. To quarter a spoonful, first divide in half lengthwise. Half spoonfuls should always be cut lengthwise because the bowl of the spoon holds more than the tip. Great care must be taken to measure accurately. Whether the quantities are exact or not often makes a difference.

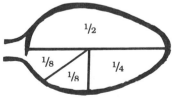

Manufacturers followed their own ideas as to the actual capacity of a "cupful" because no standard was available. In 1925, at the request of the American Home Economists Association, the U.S. Bureau of Standards and the Bureau of Home Economists investigated the situation. The result was a code of specifications that were formulated and adopted—standard measurements.

143. One-cup tin measure (left) is graduated in quarters and thirds, has a pointed green wooden handle, and pour spouts. It is 2¾" × 2⅞".

Another one-cup tin measure (right) is graduated with quarters and thirds (cup will hold more than eight ounces), has a green metal handle and pour spouts. It was probably made by Aluminum Goods Manufacturing Company and is 3" × 2⅞".

$1.25—4.50

Measuring Cups

Swans Down offered a measuring cup with a green wooden pointed handle and a copy of "New Cake Secrets" for twenty cents in 1933.

Similar to Fig. 143 is a one cup tin measure graduated at one-half and one-thirds. It has a pointed green wooden handle and is 2⅝" × 3¾".

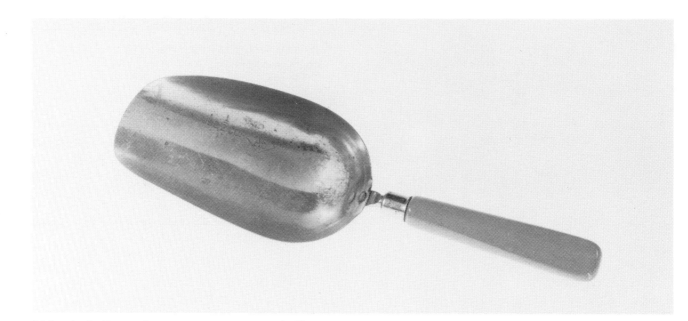

144. A & J metal scoop measures one-half cup when level. It has a green wooden handle and is 9¾″ with a 5⅜″ scoop. A & J also made this model with a red wooden handle with ivory band.

$1.50–4.50

Measuring Scoops

A scoop is a short-handled, shovel-like utensil used to measure dry ingredients.

Similar to Fig. 144 is an A & J level one-half cup metal scoop with a green wooden handle with ivory band. It is 10⅜″ with a 5⅜″ scoop.

An A & J level one-quarter cup metal scoop with a green wooden handle with ivory band is 6¾″ with a 5⅜″ scoop.

An Androck level full one-quarter cup metal scoop has a six-sided green wooden handle. It is 8⅛″ with a 3⅞″ scoop.

An Androck level full one-quarter cup metal scoop with a green wooden teardrop handle is 8″ with a 3⅞″ scoop.

A one-quarter cup and four tablespoons scoop marked WB over W has a green stained handle and is 7⅛″ with a 3⅞″ scoop.

An A & J level one-quarter cup metal scoop with a green wooden handle with ivory band was made for F. W. Woolworth Company. It is 7¼″ with a 4″ scoop.

An A & J level one-quarter cup metal scoop with a red wooden handle was also made for F. W. Woolworth Company. It is 7½″ with a 3¾″ scoop.

Measuring Spoon

The spoon has measurement markings in the bowl. A & J made a long green wooden handled spoon with a shallow metal bowl, pour spout, and measurement markings of teaspoons in the bowl. It is 12¼″ with a 4¼″ bowl.

A spoon marked EKCO U.S.A. (on bowl), Siegler (on side of handle), and Warm Floor Heaters (on other side of handle) has a red wooden handle with shallow metal bowl, pour spout, and measurement markings of teaspoons and tablespoons in the bowl. (This is a later version of the A & J.) It is 12¼″ with a 4¼″ bowl.

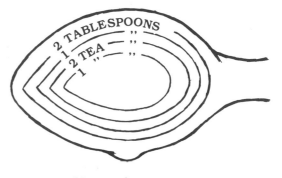

Measuring Spoon

145. The Columbia Family Scale by Landers, Frary & Clark is of green metal and has an ivory enameled metal dial. It is marked "not legal for trade, 24 pounds by ounce" and is 8⅞" × 8¼" × 6".

$4.00–24.00

Family or Household Scales

Scales weigh food placed on a platform. The weight is indicated by the pointer on a dial.

Similar to Fig. 145 is the Universal family scale by Landers, Frary & Clark. The twenty-five-pound scale is green metal, has a glass-protected white dial, and is graduated in ounces. It is 8½" × 8¼" × 5⅞".

A Continental Scale Works scale, patented September 1, 1925, has ivory metal dial protected by glass and is graduated in ounces to twenty-five pounds. It is 3⅜" × 8⅜" × 6¼".

Mixing and Cooking Tools

Batter beaters and whips are used to mix batter. Similar to Fig. 146 is a batter beater marked, "A & J BATTER BEATER–BEATER CURVED TO FIT THE BOWL." It has a four-sided red wooden handle with a 6¾" blade.

Another A & J batter beater curved to fit the bowl has a red wooden handle with ivory knob and a 6¾" blade.

A batter whip marked WB over W has a green wooden handle with black bands separated by an ivory band and a 6½" blade.

147. Androck made this spoon (left) with red wooden handle and 4¼" bowl. It is 11½".

Spoon marked PM Company (left center) has a green wooden handle with yellow tip. The nickel plated tool is 11¾" with a 3½" bowl.

This spoon (center) with a green wooden handle and no ferrule is 11¼" with a 3½" bowl.

Samson made this stainless 12⅝" steel spoon (right center) with an eight-sided, green wooden handle and 3½" bowl.

Unmarked spoon (right) with a green wooden handle with black bands separated by an ivory band is 12½" long with a 3½" bowl. **$1.50– 4.50**

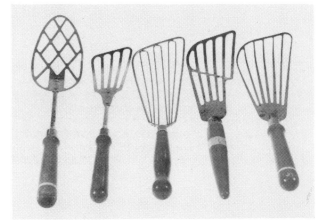

146. A & J 12¼" oval cake and batter whip (left) has a green wooden handle with ivory band and 4⅞" blade. **$2.00–3.50**

A 10¾" batter whip (left center) is marked A & J on the 4⅝" blade and Rumford Baking Powder on the green wooden handle. **$2.00–7.50**

Another unmarked tool (center) has a green wooden handle, heavy 7" wire blade, and is 11⅛" long. **$1.50–3.00**

An unmarked tool (right center) has a green wooden handle with ivory band near ferrule and measures 11¾" with a 6¾" blade. **$1.50-3.00**

An A & J batter beater (right) has a green wooden handle with ivory band and is 11⅛" with a 6¾" blade. **$1.00–3.50**

Mixing forks are curved to fit contour of bowl with angled tines for quick mixing, beating and blending.

Similar to Fig. 148 is an unmarked tool with an eight-sided green wooden handle and six tines. It is 10¼" with a 3" fork.

116

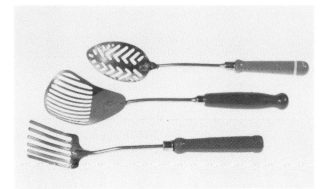

148. Foley Fork (bottom) has an eight-sided, red wooden handle and six 3″ tines. It is 10¾″ and is labeled stainless. **$1.00–3.00**

The A & J Kitchamajig™ is a red wooden handled tool that strains, drains, beats, blends, whips and mixes. It is 12¼″ long with a 4″ blade. The same tool was made with a hang-up hole and a red handle with ivory band. **$1.00–3.50**

A & J ZigZag™ mixing spoon (top), patent number 50133, has a green wooden handle with ivory band. It is chromium plated and measures 11¾″ with a 3½″ bowl. **$1.00–3.50**

149. Mixer pictured has a green wooden knob on metal lid and a clear glass tumbler graduated by ounces and cups to twelve ounces or one and one-half cups. The lid says, *Toddy mixer takes ten seconds.* The bottom says, *A meal in a glass.* Overall height is 8½″; glass is 6″ × 3″. **$1.50–3.50**

150. Drip-O-Later™ coffeepot, patent number 1,743,925, was made by the Enterprise Aluminum Company. It has a green wooden knob on lid, green wooden handle on pot, eight-cup capacity, and 11″ height. It was invented by R. F. Krause and patented January 14, 1930. The company also made a 9½″ pot with four-cup capacity. **$3.00–12.00**

Coffeepots

Coffee, the favorite breakfast beverage of millions of people, can be brewed in many different ways. Simplicity of preparation made "dripped" coffee a favorite in American homes in the 1930s.

117

151. U.S. Manufacturing Corporation made the corn popper with a green wooden handle and metal box with perforated metal lid (center). It is 26″ with a box that is 9½″× 7½″× 2⅝″.

An unmarked popper with a green wooden handle and wire box and lid (left) is 26½″ long with a box that measures 9¾″× 7⅝″× 2¼″.

Another unmarked popper (right) with a green wooden handle and metal box and wire lid is 26″ long with a box that is 9⅝″× 7⅝″× 2⅝″.

$6.50–14.00

152. Corn popper by Dominion Electrical Manufacturing Company has a metal lid with a green wooden knob on a crank handle and is 9½″× 7¾″. It operates on 110-120 volts, 500 watts.

$6.50–14.00

Corn Poppers

A corn popper has a pierced metal or wire screen box with long handle and is used to pop corn over a fire. Popping corn is said to be one of America's oldest traditions, dating back to the first Thanksgiving when the Pilgrims enjoyed it. In 1922, Montgomery Ward sold corn poppers for thirty-five cents. Sears, Roebuck sold them for thirty-nine cents in 1932.

Cooking Tools

An egg poacher, is used to cook eggs out of shells in boiling water.

A fork, an implement consisting of a handle and two or more tines, is used for piercing or stabbing food.

A funnel-strainer can be used as a funnel, a dipper, a graduated one-pint measure, a fruit jar filler, and a fine and coarse strainer.

A ladle is a long handled spoon with a deep curved bowl. Plain ladles are used to transfer or serve liquid foods such as gravy, soup, stew, or punch. Perforated ladles are used for straining.

153. This MP egg boiler, L.A. 58 (left), has a red wooden knob, collapsible handle and four-egg capacity. The base is 4″× 4″ and height is 4¼″.

The unmarked egg lifter (right) has a four-sided, green handle with ferrule and a heavy wire lifter with 2½″ depth. Length is 8″. **$2.00–5.00**

154. Unmarked egg poacher (right) is probably by Aluminum Goods Manufacturing Company. It can cook three eggs at one time, and has a spring release and a green wooden knob. **$2.50–8.00**

Unmarked egg poacher with pointed green wooden knob (left) cooks one egg and comes in three pieces. It measures 5¾″ × 3¾″. **$2.00–3.50**

155. Samson stainless steel fork (left), c. 1929, has an eight-sided, green wooden handle that is waterproof and crackproof. It measures 13⅜″ long.

This Samson stainless steel fork (second from left) is 10¼″ long and has an eight sided, green wooden handle that is waterproof and crackproof.

A & J 12⅞″ fork (third) has a green wooden handle with ivory bands, two tines, and long shank.

A & J 14½″ fork (fourth) has a green wooden handle, two tines, and short shank.

A & J 12⅝″ fork (fifth) has a green wooden handle with ivory band, short shank, three tines, and is marked chrome.

EKCO 12¾″ fork (sixth) has a red wooden handle with ivory bands, long shank, hang-up hole, and two tines.

Unmarked 13¼″ fork (seventh) is probably by A & J and has a green wooden handle with ivory band, three tines, and is of tinned wire.

Another unmarked fork (right) is probably by Androck and measures 9″. The tinned wire tool has two tines and a green teardrop handle. **$1.00–3.00**

157. A & J pouring ladle (left) has a green wooden Skyline handle and is 12¾" long with a 4¼" bowl.

An unmarked ladle with pour spouts (second from left) has a four-sided green wooden handle and measures 13¼" with a 4⅛" bowl.

Samson stainless ladle (third) has an eight-sided, green wooden handle that is waterproof and crackproof. It is 11¾" with a 3⅞" bowl.

Unmarked 12¼" slotted ladle (fourth) has a green wooden handle and 3⅛" bowl.

Chromium plated perforated ladle (fifth) was custom made for F. W. Woolworth Company by A & J and EKCO. The 10¾" ladle has a 3¾" bowl and green wooden handle with ivory band and tip.

Unmarked, nonferruled perforated ladle (sixth) has a green wooden handle and measures 12½" with a 4" bowl.

Unmarked, non-ferruled spoon (right) with a green wooden handle is 9⅛" with a 4⅛" bowl.

Soup: **$1.00—5.00**   Side pouring: **$2.00—4.50**

156. This six piece Nesco funnel has a 3¾" green metal handle and measures one quarter, one half, three quarters and one pint. It is 3⅜" × 4⅝".

$2.00—6.50

Similar to Fig. 157 is an unmarked, plain ladle with a green wooden handle and 3¾" bowl. It is 11¾" long.

Another unmarked, plain ladle with a green wooden handle with ivory band is probably by A & J. It is 11" with a 3¾" bowl.

An unmarked, plain ladle with a green wooden handle with ivory band is 11" with a 3¾" bowl.

An unmarked, plain ladle, with no ferrules, has a green wooden handle and 3¾" bowl. A spoon is used in preparing or serving food.

A turner, cake turner, lifter is incorrectly called a spatula today. It is a plain, perforated, pierced, or slotted, flat metal utensil used for flipping pancakes or turning fried eggs or chops.

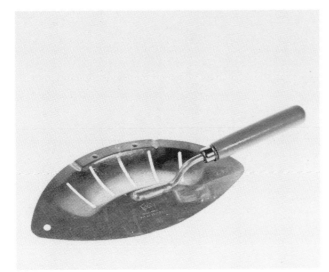

158. This Foley pan drainer, patent number 2,507,159, has a blue wooden handle and slotted metal drainer and is 11⅛"×4½". Freda I. Holmgren and Frank A. Holmgren of Minneapolis, Minnesota, were the inventors. Application was filed on April 14, 1947, and patented on May 9, 1950. They said it *can be conveniently used to drain water or liquid from kettle or sauce pan without discharging solid contents....* **$2.50–4.50**

160. This 12½" A & J spoon (left) was marked, "scraper spoon gets the corners." It has a green wooden handle and a 3¾" slotted bowl.
The same spoon (right) was made without slots and measured 12" with a 3⅞" bowl. **$1.25–4.50**

159. The Samson stainless steel basting spoon (left) has an eight-sided green wooden handle that is waterproof and crackproof. It is 12½" with a 3¾" bowl.
An A & J 11½" strainer spoon (center) has a green wooden handle and 3¾" bowl. An unmarked 11½" basting spoon (right) has a green wooden handle and 3¾" bowl. **$1.50–4.50**

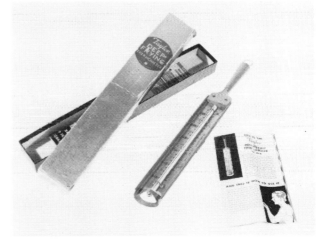

161. Taylor deep frying thermometer, c. 1933, registers from 100° to 600°. It has a green wooden handle, metal ring at top, metal pot clamp on back, and is 12½"×1⅝". The instruction book says: *This is the Taylor deep-frying thermometer No. 5910. Every housewife needs a Taylor deep-frying thermometer, for nowadays exact temperatures control good cooking and most recipes give definite temperature directions. This thermometer has an easy-reading 8-inch scale, registering from approximately 100° to 600° Fahrenheit, made of nickel silver, with handle of apple green wood. Metal ring at top for hanging. The tube is mercury-filled and has a magnifying lens. Is easily cleaned after using. Price $2.00 each. Tested and approved by Good Housekeeping Institute.* **$3.50–6.00**

162. An electric toaster made by Electrahot Manufacturing Company has green wooden handles and is 7¼″ × 7¼″ × 4¾″. It operates on 110-120 volts, 500 watts. **$5.00—12.00**

164. A three-blade lifter was made by Gadget Manufacturing, patent number 2,063,432, and measures 12½″ with a 6½″ blade. **$5.00—10.00**

This was invented by Minnie Greene and Lois Udey of El Segundo, California. Application was filed August 16, 1935, and patent granted December 8, 1936, patent number 2,063,432. They said: *This invention relates to improvements in kitchen utensils and has particular reference to an implement adapted for use in lifting meats or fowls from pans or roasters, in turning cakes, and other varied uses in culinary art. The principal object of the invention is to provide means whereby the certain blades of the device are movable or adjustable with relation to a third stationary blade, thus increasing the lifting area of the implement, so as to permit the same to be readily adapted for use in lifting food products or the like of different sizes and varying dimensions. . . .*

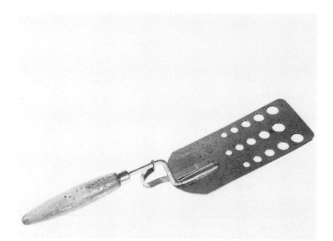

163. This is three-blade lifter (Fig. 164) in closed position.

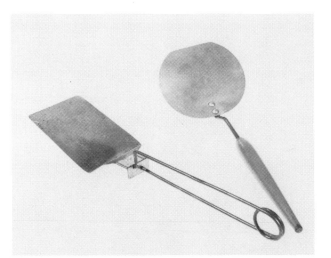

165. A & J made this plain flip turner (left) so the operator could squeeze handles together to flip turner. It has a green metal handle and is 13″ with a 5¾″ blade.

Unmarked 13″ turner (right) has a green wooden handle with no ferrules and a 4″ blade. **$1.25—5.00**

166. A & J made a perforated 13″ turner (left) with white wooden handle and made a similar one with a green, non-ferruled handle.

This A & J (left center) slotted turner has a green wooden handle, 4¾″ blade and 13¼″ length.

Androck made a 13½″ turner (center) with a red wooden handle and a 4¾″ slotted blade.

Unmarked 11¾″ turner (right center) has a green wooden handle and a 6″ perforated blade.

Another unmarked 14″ turner (right) has a green wooden handle with no ferrule and a 4½″ perforated blade.　　　　　　　　　　　　**$1.25–5.00**

167. White Cross™ waffle iron (left) by National Stamping & Electric Works was patented November 28, 1922, October 26, 1923, and April 21, 1925. It has three green wooden handles and is 5½″ high with a 7¼″ waffle area.

Unmarked electric waffle iron (right) is either an individual waffle iron or a toy one. It has a green wooden knob, is 3¼″ high, and has a waffle area of 4⅝″.　　　　　　　　　　　　**$4.00–8.50**

Sifters and Strainers

A sifter is a sieve with a mechanized action for forcing flour or powdered sugar through the mesh to aerate it to produce a standard measure.

Rotary Sifter

A crank rotates wire or blade agitators over convex wire mesh in a rotary sifter.

Similar to Fig. 168 is Bromwell's measuring-sifter for two, three, four and five cups, patent number 1,753,995. It has green wooden handle and crank and four-wire agitator. It is 6¼″ × 5¼″.

Bromwell also made this model with a red wooden handle and crank.

Bromwell made the same sifter with a metal handle.

A Bromwell measuring-sifter for one, two, and three cups has a green wooden crank, metal handle and two-wire agitator. It is 5⅝″ × 4½″.

A later version carried patent number 1,753,995.

Bromwell's Bee™, patent number 1,753,995, was a green metal sifter with black wooden crank, metal handle, and two-wire agitator. It is 5⅝″ × 4½″. This same sifter was also made with a green wooden crank.

An Acme sifter with a green wooden crank, metal handle, and three-blade agitator was probably made by National Enameling & Stamping. It is 6¼″ × 5¼″.

The Nesco one-cup sifter made by National Enameling & Stamping has a green wooden crank, metal handle, and wire agitator. It is 3½″ × 3″.

An unmarked sifter with a blue wooden handle and crank has a four-wire agitator and is 6⅜″ × 5⅛″.

168. This XXX extra heavy Bromwell's sifter (left) has a green wooden handle and crank and a four-wire agitator. It is 6¼″×5¼″. The Bromwell's measuring-sifter (right), patent number 1,753,995, is guaranteed to measure two, three, four and five cups. It has a green wooden crank, metal handle, two-wire agitator and measures 6¼″×5¼″. The Bromwell flour sifter was invented by George G. Melish of Cincinnati, Ohio. Application was filed June 18, 1926, and patent granted April 8, 1930. He was assignor to the Bromwell Wire Goods Company, Cincinnati, Ohio. He said it *is designed with an object to produce a construction of extreme simplicity necessitating a minimum of material and manufacturing operation, thereby reducing the cost of production and consequent sale price without destroying the efficiency with which a flour sifter should function.* . . .

$1.50–6.00

April 8, 1930.   T. G. MELISH   1,753,995

FLOUR SIFTER

Filed June 18, 1926

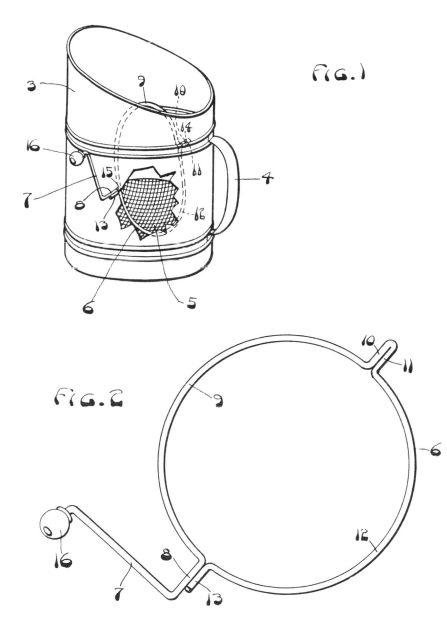

FIG. 1

FIG. 2

INVENTOR
Thomas G. Melish
BY Thornton Bogert
ATTORNEY

169.   This patent drawing is of a flour sifter.

170. The Fred J. Meyers Manufacturing Company made the Hunter's sifter, "standard of the world," with a green wooden crank, horizontal metal handle, and four-wire agitator. It is 6⅜"×5". **$2.50—5.00**

Similar to Fig. 170 is an Improved Genuine sifter with green wooden end and crank knob, horizontal metal handle, and four-wire agitator. It is 6¼" × 5¼".

A Special High Grade Paragon Flour Sifter™ made of extra heavy tin has a green wooden crank knob, horizontal metal handle, and four-wire agitator. It is 6⅜" × 5¼".

Horizontal Sifter

This shaker type sifter has back and forth action.

Trigger Action Sifter

To sift flour, squeeze handles. This type of sifter could be operated with one hand, leaving the other hand free to hold measuring cup or to stir the batter.

Similar to Fig. 173 is the SAVORY "JUNIOR"™, tested & approved, serial 2659, Good Housekeeping Institute, *Good Housekeeping magazine*. It has green metal bands and is 4¾" × 4".

The Foley five-cup sifter has a blue metal handle and is 5" × 5½".

171. Bromwell's multiple sifter (left) has lids on both ends, green wooden handle, and reversible sifter. It is 7"×5" and will sift flour as often as desired.
$2.50—5.00

Bromwell's duet, two-screen sifter (center) has a horizontal green wooden handle and measures 3"×3½".
$2.50—5.00

A Duplex™ five-cup sifter by Uneek Utilities Corporation, patent 1922 (right) has a flat wire agitator and horizontal, green wooden handle. It is 6¾"×6". The company also made a similar sifter with a horizontal blue handle. **$5.00—12.00**

172. This electric flour sifter was made by Miracle Products, Inc. It has a blue wooden handle and ivory metal sifter, and it is 5"×4⅜". Directions say "do not immerse in water, Cat. No. 5-1 A.C. only, 110 volts, 60 cycle, .5 ampere."

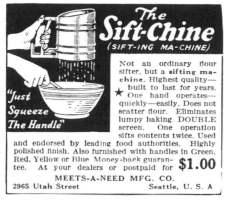
173.

174. The Sift Chine™ sifter (left) has a green metal handle and measures 5⅞" × 5⅛". *Good Housekeeping* in 1929 said: *The SIFT-CHINE (Sift-ing Machine) "just squeeze the handle." Not an ordinary flour sifter, but a sifting machine. Highest quality—built to last for years. One hand operates—quickly—easily. Does not scatter flour. Eliminates lumpy baking. Double screen. One operation sifts contents twice. Used and endorsed by leading food authorities. Highly polished finish. Also furnished with handles in green, red, yellow, or blue. Money-back guarantee. At your dealers or postpaid for $1.00. Meets-A-Need Mfg. Co. 2965 Utah Street, Seattle, U.S.A.* **$3.25—5.50**

A metal trigger flour sifter (right) measures 7⅝" × 7¼". Label reads: *Level Measurement-Foley Sifter-Aluminum-Sift Into Cup. Tested and approved Good Housekeeping Institute. Be Foley equipped with food mill, chopper, fork, can opener made by Foley Manufacturing Co. Minneapolis 13, Minn. Sifts directly into measuring cup, eliminating extra handling of flour. Measurement is leveled by resting bottom of sifter on edge of cup and circling cup. Patent Pending.* **$1.50—4.50**

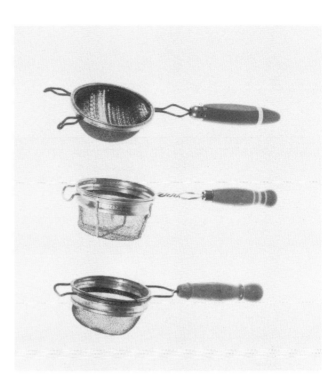

175. Ajax heavy duty strainer, patent number 2,006,566, (top) has a red wooden handle with ivory band and measures 8½" × 2½". Myron J. Zimmer of Chicago, Illinois, invented this strainer, which was filed on January 11, 1934, patented July 24, 1935, and assigned to Edward Katzinger Company.

Androck made this tool with removable strainer (center), c. 1930. It has green wooden handle with three ivory bands and ferrule, flat bottom, and wire supports. It is 7½" × 2½".

Androck made another removable strainer (bottom), patent number 1,874,410. It has a green wooden handle and is 7½" × 2¼". The inventor was Charles Andrews, Rockford, Illinois, assignor to the Washburn Company. He filed on August 9, 1930, and patent was granted in 1932.   **$1.50—3.50**

Tea and Coffee Strainers

Strainers are used to separate liquids from solids by pouring through wire mesh.

Similar to Fig. 175 is Androck patent number 1,874,410 with a blue with ivory tip, six-sided wooden handle and removable strainer. It measures 7½" × 2¼".

An unmarked strainer with a green wooden handle has a removable strainer and is 7¾" × 2¾".

A one-piece strainer by Ekco and A & J has a four-sided, red with ivory band wooden handle with a ferrule and hang-up hole. The bottom is flat. It is 8¾" × 3¼".

EKCO and A & J also made a similar strainer that was 8¼" × 2¾".

127

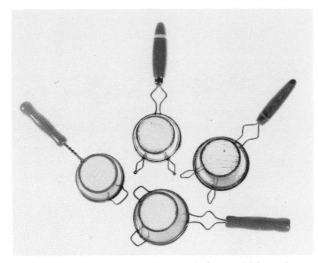

176. A & J made this strainer (left) c. 1932. It has a green wooden handle, green metal wall and is attached with twisted wire. It is 7³/₈" × 2¹/₂". Strainer (top), also by A & J has green handle with ivory band.

Miracle Gem™ strainer (right) has a red wooden handle and red metal wall with white pictures of a teapot, coffeepot, and cup. It measures 7⁵/₈" × 2³/₄".

A strainer which was given away with Salada tea (bottom) has a green wooden handle and green metal wall. It measures 7³/₄" × 2³/₄". Strainers have solid metal walls with removable strainers. **$1.50—3.50**

177. Androck strainer (top), patent number 1,874,410, has a six-sided, green wooden handle which is removable. It measures 9" × 3³/₈".

Another Androck strainer with the same patent number (center) has a green teardrop wooden handle, ferrule and removable strainer. It is 8¹/₂" × 3¹/₄".

A one-piece strainer by EKCO and A & J (bottom) has an ivory banded, red wooden handle, ferrule, hang-up hole, and measures 8³/₄" × 3¹/₄".
$1.50—3.50

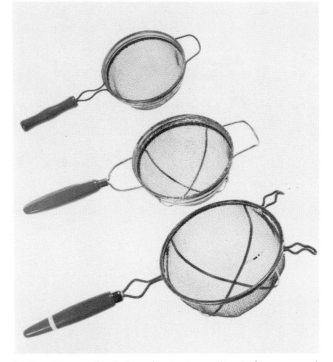

178. Unmarked bowl strainer (top) has a red wooden handle and removable strainer. It measures 9³/₄" × 4¹/₄".

Androck strainer (center), patent number 1,874,410, has a six-sided, green wooden handle and removable strainer with wire supports. It measures 12" × 5". Androck made a similar strainer that was 14¹/₂" × 6".

A & J Ajax™ heavy duty strainer (bottom), patent number 2,006,566 has an ivory banded, red Skyline wooden handle with ferrule. The one-piece strainer, c. 1936, has wire supports and is 14" × 6".
$3.00—6.00

Similar to Fig. 176 is an strainer with a four-sided, green with ivory band wooden handle and ferrule. It has a green metal wall and is 8" × 2¹/₄".

A strainer marked Con'l Gem Company has a green wooden handle, green metal wall, ferrule and measures 8¹/₄" × 3¹/₄".

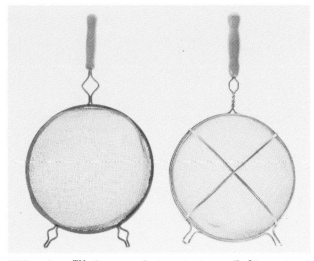

179. Ajax™ heavy duty strainer (left), patent number 2,006,566, is a one-piece preserving strainer by A & J. It has a green wooden handle and measures 15¾″×8½″.

Androck removable strainer with wire supports (right) has a green wooden handle and 15″×8″ size.
$3.00–6.00

Other Kitchen Specialties

A variety of kitchen items, not fitting into any other grouping, range from brushes to the very important fly swatter (a must for every home) and carpet beaters. Curling irons, handirons, plungers, and dish mops are also found here.

(continued)

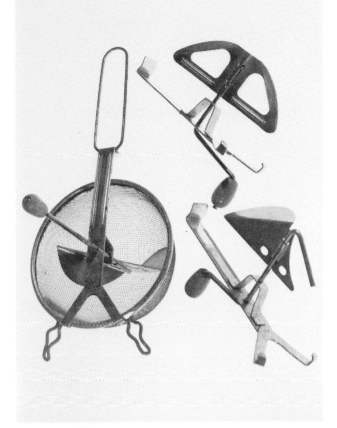

180. Ajax™ heavy duty strainer by A & J (top) is marked with patent number 2,006,566. It has a metal handle, a one-piece revolving strainer, and measures 14″×6″. The rotator has metal blades and clamps to the strainer. A green wooden crank knob is used to turn the 5½″ blades to sift dry ingredients and also to mash or puree fruits and vegetables.

Another A & J revolving strainer (right) has an open, double-wing blade measuring 5⅜″. It also features a metal clamp and green wooden crank knob.

A & J strainer (left) with single wing, metal clamp, and green wooden crank knob measures 7¾″ with a 4⅜″ blade.　　Complete strainer: **$3.50–5.00**
Blade, no strainer: **$1.00–3.50**

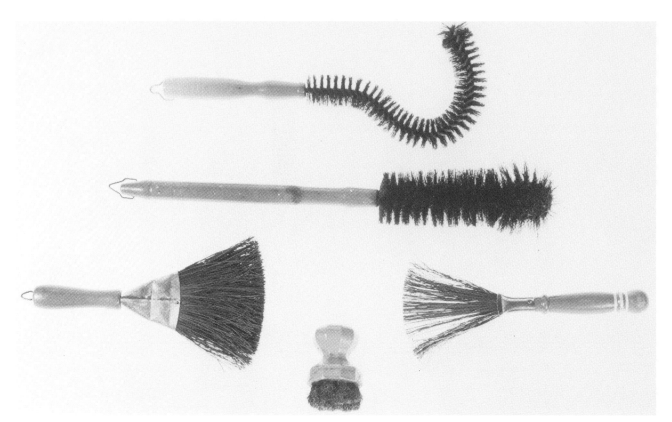

181. Unmarked glass coffee maker brush (top), c. 1936, is used to reach and clean every part of the glass bowl. It has a metal hanger, black Chinese bristles, green wooden 5″ handle, and 11¼″ length.

Unmarked 15″ milk bottle brush (center), c. 1936, has black Chinese bristles, 9″ green wooden handle, and a metal hanger.

This 8″ unmarked sink brush (left), c. 1930, has a green wooden handle, corn stock, metal hanger, and 4¼″×3″ brush. It was used to sweep crumbs out of the sink.

Unmarked sink brush, probably by Androck (right)

has a green wooden handle with three ivory bands and ferrule. It is 8⅛″ with a 4¼″×3″ metal brush. This was sold in conjunction with a small shovel and a perforated metal three-sided sink rack that fits in the corner of the sink. It was used to clean soapstone and cast iron sinks without wetting hands.

This unmarked utility brush (bottom) sold for ten cents in 1939. It has a ten-sided, green wooden knob handle and fine brass wire brush measuring ¾″×1¾″. It is used to scour pots and pans.
$1.00—4.00

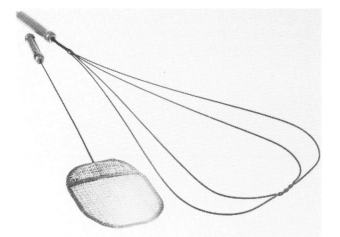

182. Unmarked 29″ carpet or upholstery beater (right) has a green wooden handle, four wires, wire hanger, and 4⅞″ handle.   **$6.00—16.00**

The unmarked fly swatter (left) is made of woven fiber and cellophane. It is 23¼″ long with a 6½″× 4¾″ swatter.

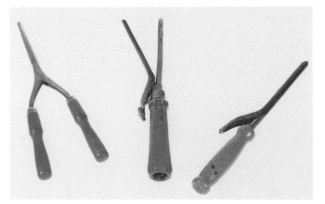

183. This curling iron (left) has green wooden, ferruled handles which measure 3¾″. Overall length is 9½″.

Unmarked electric curling iron (center) has a plastic cool button, 4″ handle and eight-sided, green wooden handle. It is 9¾″.

Another curling iron (right) has a 4″ green wooden handle and is 9¾″. The green plastic cool button on the clamp is missing.   Electric: **$2.00—10.00**
Non-electric: **$1.00—15.00**

184. This unmarked dipper (left) has a ten-sided, green wooden handle and is 14³/₄″ × 4⁷/₈″.

Unmarked dish mop (left center) has 15¢ stamped in ink on the red wooden handle. The 3¹/₄″ mop is cotton yarn, and total length is 12″.

Plunger marked Daisy Force Cup Number 4™ (center) has a green wooden handle and brown rubber cup. It is 11″ × 4″. The Daisy Number 400 is a similar model.

An unmarked, green wooden pot cover knob (top, center right) has a metal washer and screw. Five 1″ knobs sold for five cents in 1936.

This Surehold™ utensil cleaner (bottom, right center) by Select Specialties Company, has a green wooden handle with ferrule and a metal clamp with serrated teeth. The serrated teeth held steel wool while cleaning utensils. It is 5¹/₂″ × 1³/₈″. A similar tool with red handle was also made.

This "whatsit" (top right) has a red wooden handle with ferrule and a stainless steel scoop with thumb rest. Length is 6¹/₄″, and scoop measures 2³/₈″ × 1¹/₂″.

Another "whatsit" (bottom right) has a red wooden handle with ferrule and flat metal blade with three serrated cutting edges. Length is 5″, and blade is 1³/₈″ × 2″. A similar tool with a mustard colored handle was also made. **$1.00—6.00**

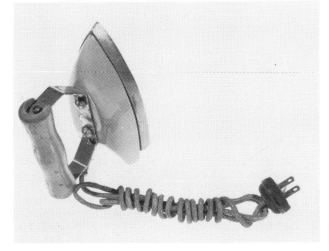

185. Unmarked iron has a green wooden handle, green metal base, and metal iron surface. It is 6″ × 3″ × 4″. **$4.00—9.00**

131

Toy Kitchen Collectibles

Toy kitchen items are becoming popular collectibles. It is hard to trace many of them, because so few manufacturers marked these products. Most of the kitchen articles were ordinary toys.

Mother's Little Helper™ juvenile kitchen tools were introduced in April, 1923, by the A & J Manufacturing Company of Binghamton, New York. Johnson, one of the founders of the company, hoped that the A & J name would become so familiar that when children (the future bakers and homemakers) grew up they would buy A & J products. A & J kitchen utensils were not toys but exact miniature replicas of regular A & J products. These juvenile items continued to be manufactured until 1937.

Other kitchen toy collectibles include an unmarked, collapsible ironing board with natural wooden board and green wooden legs. It measures 29¾" × 7¾" × 17". Also, an unmarked electric waffle iron has a green wooden knob and is 3¼" high with a 4⅝" waffle area. Figs. 191-195 show A & J juvenile kitchen tools.

186.   The two toy beaters by A & J (left) have colored wooden handles, metal cranks, and four wings. They are 5⅝" long and were patented October 9, 1923.

Two Betty Taplin eggbeaters (center) have red wooden cranks, metal handles, and four wings. The beater on the left has a metal lid (bowl missing) and is 5½" × 2⅞". The other beater is 5½".

Beater: **$2.00—8.00**
Betty Taplin and other marked beaters: **$5.50—9.00**

A toy beater by Criterion (second from right) has a red wooden handle and crank, four wings, and 5⅛" length.

A 4½" beater marked Bal-so on the shaft (right) has a red wooden handle and crank and four wings. A similar beater which is unmarked was also made.

Betty Taplin beater and
lid (bowl missing): **$1.50—15.00**

187. The candy container (top left) has a clear glass lantern, wire handle, and green pierced metal lid (for salt or pepper). It measures 4¾"× 1¾". The bottom is marked: "gelatin, sugar, starch, corn syrup, ½ oz. certified U.S. colors; Jeannette, Pa. T. H. Stough Co." **$2.00–5.00**

Unmarked electric percolator coffeepot (right) has a red wooden handle and measures 6¾"× 3⅜". **$3.50–7.00**

Unmarked tin cookie cutters (below coffeepot) are in the shape of a chicken (2¼") and a rabbit (2¾"). **$2.00–15.00**

Fagley made these junior card party cutters (front center) which sold at the Frank P. Hall Company hardware store for nineteen cents per set (boxed) in March, 1926. All are unmarked metal cutters. The spade is 2"; diamond is 2⅛"; club is 1⅞". **$2.00–3.50**

The unmarked wire dish drainer (top center) is 8¾"× 6¼". **$1.50–6.00**

Unmarked metal muffin tin (top right) measures 6½"× 4¼". **$1.25–2.50**

An iron marked Utility Iron V. 80 W. (top left) has a green wooden handle and green metal base with metal iron surface and rest. Its dimensions are 5⅝"× 3"× 4". **$4.00–10.00**

A Sunny Suzy™ iron by Wolverine (front left) has a red metal base with metal iron surface and black plastic handle. It measures 5¼"× 2⅝"× 2¾". **$2.00–6.00**

An unmarked metal measuring cup (left of irons) is graduated from one-quarter cup to one teaspoon. It has a red metal handle and measures 1¾"× 1¾". **$1.00–2.50**

The three unmarked rolling pins (in drainer) have colored wooden handles, 4" rollers, and are about 8" long. **$2.00–9.00**

A strainer spoon (in drainer) has a red wooden handle, no ferrule, 2¼" bowl, and length of 7⅝". **$2.50–4.00**

An unmarked perforated skimmer (in drainer) has a red wooden handle, no ferrule, and measures 8¼"× 2¼". **$2.50–4.00**

188. A & J sold toy kitchen tools which were replicas of adult-sized tools.

189. A & J tools pictured have white wooden handles with blue tips. They are (from left), 2¼″ man cookie cutter; 2¼″ rabbit cookie cutter (A & J juvenile cookie cutters are marked, which is unusual for most cookie cutters); 7⅛″ fork with two 3⅝″ tines and gray rather than blue tip; 6½″ ladle with 2″ bowl; 6⅝″ unmarked potato masher with 2″×2⅞″ masher; 5⅜″ paring knife with 2⅜″ blade; unmarked 9″ rolling pin with 4¼″ roller; 7½″ measuring spoon (marked full teaspoon half teaspoon) with 2¼″ bowl and white wooden handle; 8″ slotted spoon with 2½″ bowl; 8⅛″ unmarked spatula with 5⅛″ blade; and 8⅜″ turner with 2⅝″ blade.

A & J cookie cutters: **$3.50 up**
Fork or paring knife: **$2.00—4.50**
Potato masher: **$2.50—6.00**
Rolling pin: **$2.00—9.00**
Ladle, spoons: **$3.00—4.50**
Spatula, turner: **$2.00—4.50**

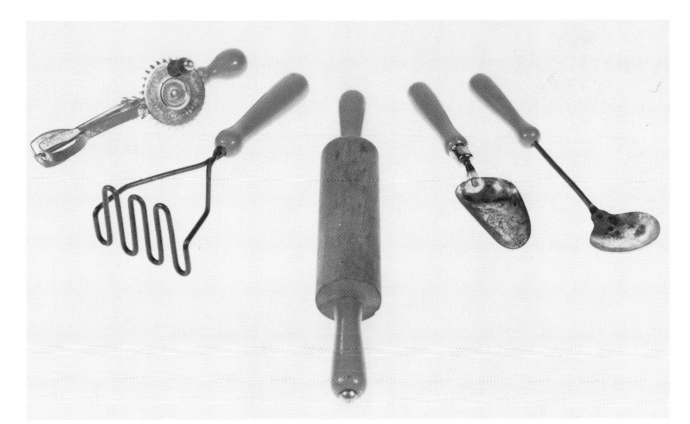

190. These A & J tools have green wooden handles.
They are (from left): beater with four wings and
wooden crank handle and knob; 6³/8″ unmarked
potato masher with four loops and 2¹/4″ width; 9″
unmarked rolling pin with 4¹/4″ roller; 2¹/8″ × 1¹/4″
scoop with length of 5¹/2″; and 6⁷/8″ measuring spoon
with 2¹/4″ bowl marked full teaspoon half teaspoon.

As toys become more collectible, the prices are rising.

Iron: **$3.00–8.50**
Rolling pin: **$2.00–9.00**
Spatula or turner: **$2.00–4.50**
Strainer spoon: **$3.00–4.00**
Complete set: **$20.00–25.00**

191.

135

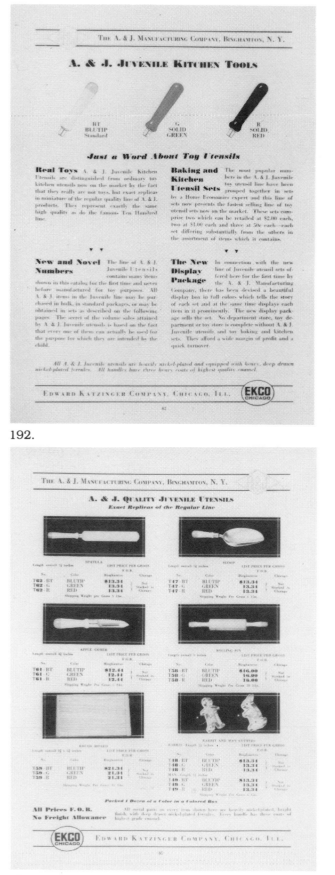
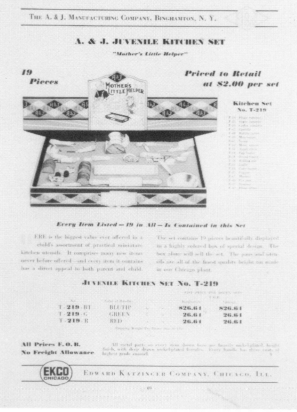

Where Do We Go From Here?

Related to the era of colorful kitchens and gadgets from 1920 to 1950 are many other fascinating kinds of kitchen collectibles. Large kitchen furniture or equipment items, including the all-purpose cabinets, storage units, work tables, kitchen tables and chairs, iceboxes, and stoves are being sought.

Small appliances such as irons, toasters, and waffle irons and cooking equipment, which include bakeware, enamelware, and aluminumware, are other options to collectors.

There is a large selection of gadgets with metal handles for a variety of uses. These did not add a touch of color and in some instances were not as easy to hold as the wood handled gadgets, but the metal handles were more durable. Also of interest are the gadgets still packaged as they were originally marketed, which make them informative and colorful.

Old grocery store items offer collectors much variety. Tins of spices, coffee, crackers, and lard; bottles of syrup and condiments; packages or boxes of staples, matches, and cheese, and many more too numerous to mention are colorful and attractive to display.

Cookbooks and booklets give recipes, household hints, and interesting pictures and illustrations. Giveaway or premium booklets—from manufacturers advertising an array of products—are also informative and representative of the era.

All kinds and colors of depression glass, dishes, and dinnerware such as FIESTAWARE™ are other aspects of collectibles from 1920 to 1950.

These items are not necessarily the most beautiful collectibles, but certainly they can be among the most useful.

Where do we stop? As you can see there are many facets of collecting which relate to the kitchen. The choice is limited only by whatever appeals to you. Happy hunting!

Bibliography

A & J Manufacturing Company, Binghamton, New York, and Edward Katzinger Company, Chicago, Illinois. Catalogs: 1930, 1932, 1935-1941, 1947-1950.

American Home. New York, New York: Country Life-American Home Corporation, American Home Corporation (later), 1920-1945, monthly.

Antique Trader. Dubuque, Iowa: Babka Publishing Company, weekly.

Baird, James, ed. *Cook's Catalogue.* New York, New York; Evanston, Illinois; San Francisco, California; London, England: Harper and Row, 1975.

Better Homes and Gardens. Des Moines, Iowa: Meredith Publishing Company, 1918-1948, monthly.

The W. Bingham Company, Cleveland, Ohio, Number 37. Catalog.

Burris-Meyers, Elizabeth. *Decorating Livable Homes.* New York, New York: Prentice Hall, 1937.

Conran, Terrence. *The Kitchen Book.* New York, New York: Crown Publishers Inc., 1977.

Cosentino, Geraldine, and Stewart, Regina. *Kitchenware — A Handbook of Collectibles — A Guide for the Beginning Collector.* Racine, Wisconsin: Stewart Golden Press Inc., 1977.

Country Gentleman. Philadelphia, Pennsylvania: Curtis Publishing Company, 1930-1937, monthly.

Ross Crane Book of Home Furnishing and Decoration. Chicago, Illinois: Fred J. Drake and Co., 1925.

Crowley, Ellen T., ed. *Trade Name Dictionary.* 2nd ed. Madison Heights, Michigan: Gale Research Co., 1979.

Ewen, Stuart. *Captains of Consciousness; Advertising and the Social Roots of the Consumer Culture.* New York, New York: McGraw-Hill, 1976.

Fischer, Katherine A., Director. *Good Meals and How to Plan Them.* Good Housekeeping Institute, 1927.
_____.*Good Meals and How to Prepare Them.* Good Housekeeping Institute, 1927.

Franklin, Linda Campbell. *From Hearth to Cookstove — Collectibles of the American Kitchen 1700-1930.* Florence, Alabama: House of Collectibles, 1975.

General Foods Corporation. *All About Home Baking.* New York, New York, 1937.

Giedion, Sigfried. *Mechanization Takes Command, A Contribution to Anonymous History.* New York, New York: Oxford University Press, 1948.

Good Housekeeping. New York, New York: Good Housekeeping, 1918-1948, monthly.

Grossinger, Tania. *The Great Gadget Catalogue.* New York, New York: Grosset and Dunlap Publishers, 1977.

Harrison, Molly. *The Kitchen in History.* New York, New York: Charles Scribner's Sons, 1972.

Hill, Janet McKenzie, compiled. *The Rumford Way of Cookery and Household Economy.* Providence, Rhode Island: Rumford Company.

House and Garden. New York, New York: Conde Nast Publications, 1920-1945, monthly.

House Beautiful. New York, New York: Field Publications, 1920-1940, monthly.

Household. Topeka, Kansas: Arthur Capper, publisher, various issues from 1927-1937, monthly.

Ladies' Home Journal. Philadelphia, Pennsylvania: Curtis Publishing Company, 1930-1945, monthly.

Lantz, Louise K. *Old American Kitchenware 1725-1925.* Camden, New Jersey, and Hanover, Pennsylvania: T. Nelson and Everybody's Press, 1970.
_____.*Revised Price Guide to Old American Kitchenware.* Hydes, Maryland: Louise K. Lantz, 1972.

Lebhar, Godfrey M. *Chain Stores in America: 1859-1962.* New York, New York: Lebhar-Friedman, 1963.

Lifshey, Earl. *The Housewares Story — A History of the American Housewares Industry.* Chicago, Illinois: National Housewares Manufacturers Association, 1973.

Lynes, Russell. *The Domesticated Americans.* New York, New York: Harper and Row Publishers, 1957, 1963.

Matthews, Mary Lou. *American Kitchen Collectibles Identification and Price Guide.* Gas City, Indiana: L-W Promotions, 1973.

Montgomery Ward Catalog. Chicago, Illinois: Montgomery Ward Company, 1922.

Novak, Mary. *Kitchen Antiques.* New York, New York: Praeger, 1975.

Ohio Antique Review. Worthington, Ohio: Ohio Antique Review Inc., monthly.

Revi, Albert Christian, ed. *Spinning Wheel's Antiques for Women.* Secaucus, New Jersey: Castle Books, 1974.
_____.*The Spinning Wheel's Complete Book of Antiques.* New York, New York: Grosset and Dunlap Publishers, 1977.

Rutt, Anna H. *Home Furnishing.* New York, New York: John Wiley and Sons Inc., 1935.

Scull, Penrose. *From Peddlars to Merchant Princes — A history of selling in America.* Chicago, Illinois; New York, New York: Follett Publishing Company, 1967.

Sears, Roebuck and Company, catalogs. Chicago, Illinois: Sears, Roebuck and Company, 1920-1945.

Sherwood, Ruth F. *Homes Today and Tomorrow.* Peoria, Illinois: Charles A. Bennett Company Inc., 1972.

Smallzried, Kathleen Ann. *The Everlasting Pleasure, Influences on American Kitchens, Cooks and Cooking from 1565 to 2000,* New York, New York: Appleton Century Crofts, Inc., 1956.

Smith Bros. Hardware Company, Columbus, Ohio, Cut Easy Catalog No. 51. Columbus, Ohio: Smith Brothers.

Spinning Wheel. Hanover, Pennsylvania: Everybody's Press, monthly.

Splint, Sarah Field. *The Art of Cooking and Serving.* Cincinnati, Ohio: Proctor and Gamble, 1928.

Steinmetz, Rollin C. *History of the American Kitchen 1776-1976.* Kreamer, Snyder County, Pennsylvania: Wood-Mode Cabinetry, 1975.

The Story of the Washburn Company and of Its Associated Companies. Worcester, Massachusetts: Washburn Company, 1960.

Time-Life Books, ed. *Time-Life Books, This Fabulous Century,* 1920-1930, 1930-1940. New York, New York: Time Inc., 1969.

Toulouse, Julian Harrison. *Fruit Jars, a Collector's Manual.* Camden, New Jersey, and Hanover, Pennsylvania: Everybodys-Nelson Press, 1969.

U.S. Patent Office Official Gazette. Washington, D.C.: U.S. Government Printing Office, 1918-1950, weekly.

Weil, Gordon L. *Sears, Roebuck, U.S.A. — The Great American Catalog Store and How It Grew.* Briarcliff Manor, New York, New York: Stein and Day, 1977.

Women's Home Companion. New York, New York, and Springfield, Ohio: Crowell and Collier Company, monthly.

The George Worthington Company catalogs: 1936, 1941. Cleveland, Ohio: George Worthington Company.

Index

Illustrations of items are indicated by boldface type.

About the Author

Meet a woman who took a nickel-and-dime hobby and found so much fascination in her collection she developed a comprehensive and definitive book for other collectors of kitchen nostalgia. Jane Celehar was born in Atlantic City, New Jersey, and raised in nearby Margate. A graduate of the University of Pennsylvania in Philadelphia, she is a registered dental hygienist.

She enjoys bridge and cooking from "scratch," is at ease with crewel needlework, and has a flair for decorating. The hours she enjoys with several antiques groups take priority in her varied schedule. She appreciates fine craftsmanship and the investment of time in projects of lasting value. Her present home in Ohio reflects these qualities.

Jane and husband John made their home in Reading, Massachusetts, and raised their three children, Karen, Georgia, and Leo. Deeply involved in the community, Jane was president of the League of Women Voters, an active participant on the Bicentennial Commission, and an elected library trustee.

For years, the Celehars have collected antiques, furnishing their home with pine and cherry country furniture with an emphasis on kitchenware. They vastly extended their kitchen collection by recognizing future "treasures" in items of the more recent past.

An avid reader, Jane is at home in the library, but her search for information about her "green

handled" kitchen tools proved frustrating. The book which would provide the information she sought had not been printed. What else to do but write it herself?

The resources the author needed to tap reached beyond bookshelves and cross-reference files to people whose interests and memories were vital to this project. The result? *Kitchens and Gadgets, 1920 to 1950.*